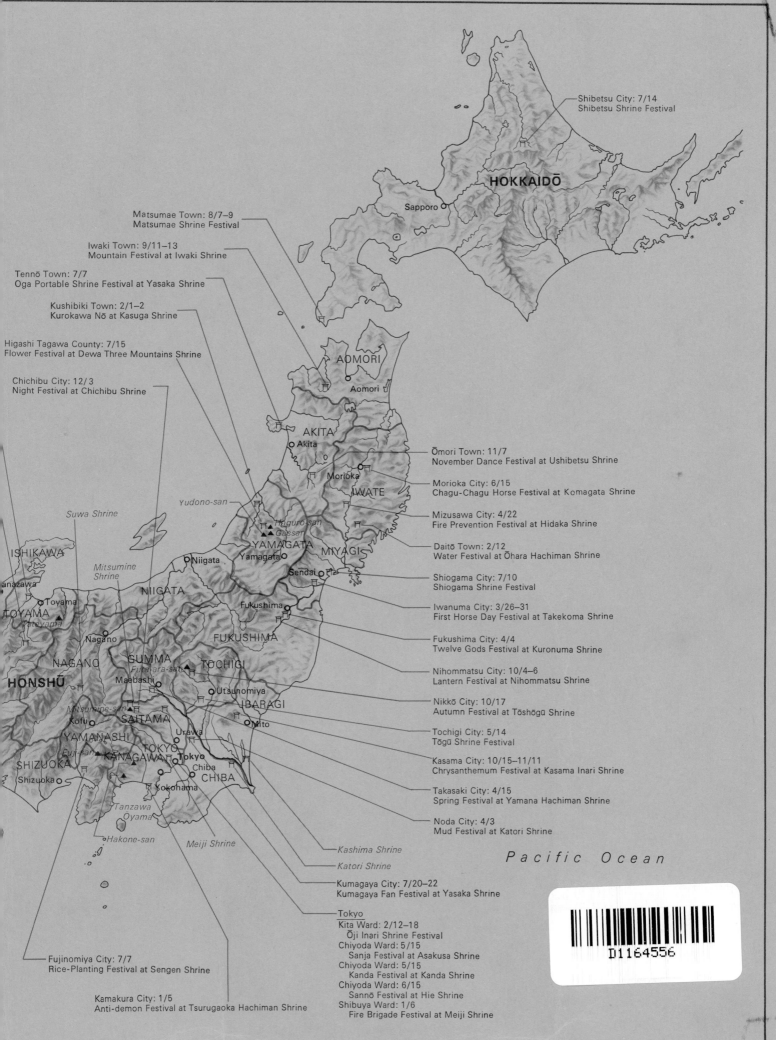

Shibetsu City: 7/14
Shibetsu Shrine Festival

HOKKAIDŌ

Sapporo

Matsumae Town: 8/7–9
Matsumae Shrine Festival

Iwaki Town: 9/11–13
Mountain Festival at Iwaki Shrine

Tennō Town: 7/7
Oga Portable Shrine Festival at Yasaka Shrine

Kushibiki Town: 2/1–2
Kurokawa Nō at Kasuga Shrine

Higashi Tagawa County: 7/15
Flower Festival at Dewa Three Mountains Shrine

Chichibu City: 12/3
Night Festival at Chichibu Shrine

AOMORI

Aomori

AKITA

Akita

Morioka

IWATE

Ōmori Town: 11/7
November Dance Festival at Ushibetsu Shrine

Morioka City: 6/15
Chagu-Chagu Horse Festival at Komagata Shrine

Mizusawa City: 4/22
Fire Prevention Festival at Hidaka Shrine

Daitō Town: 2/12
Water Festival at Ōhara Hachiman Shrine

Shiogama City: 7/10
Shiogama Shrine Festival

Iwanuma City: 3/26–31
First Horse Day Festival at Takekoma Shrine

Fukushima City: 4/4
Twelve Gods Festival at Kuronuma Shrine

Nihommatsu City: 10/4–6
Lantern Festival at Nihommatsu Shrine

Nikkō City: 10/17
Autumn Festival at Tōshōgū Shrine

Tochigi City: 5/14
Tōgū Shrine Festival

Kasama City: 10/15–11/11
Chrysanthemum Festival at Kasama Inari Shrine

Takasaki City: 4/15
Spring Festival at Yamana Hachiman Shrine

Noda City: 4/3
Mud Festival at Katori Shrine

Yudono-san

Suwa Shrine

Haguro-san
Gassan
YAMAGATA
Yamagata

MIYAGI

Sendai

Mitsumine
Shrine

ISHIKAWA

anazawa

Toyama

TOYAMA
Tateyama

Niigata

NIIGATA

Fukushima

FUKUSHIMA

Nagano

NAGANO

GUMMA
Futara-san

TOCHIGI

HONSHŪ

Maebashi

Utsunomiya

Mitsumine-san

Kōfu

SAITAMA

Urawa

IBARAGI

Mito

YAMANASHI

Fuji-san

TOKYO

KANAGAWA

Tokyo

Chiba

CHIBA

SHIZUOKA

Shizuoka

Yokohama

Tanzawa
Oyama

Hakone-san

Meiji Shrine

Kashima Shrine

Katori Shrine

Kumagaya City: 7/20–22
Kumagaya Fan Festival at Yasaka Shrine

Tokyo
Kita Ward: 2/12–18
    Ōji Inari Shrine Festival
Chiyoda Ward: 5/15
    Sanja Festival at Asakusa Shrine
Chiyoda Ward: 5/15
    Kanda Festival at Kanda Shrine
Chiyoda Ward: 6/15
    Sannō Festival at Hie Shrine
Shibuya Ward: 1/6
    Fire Brigade Festival at Meiji Shrine

Fujinomiya City: 7/7
Rice-Planting Festival at Sengen Shrine

Kamakura City: 1/5
Anti-demon Festival at Tsurugaoka Hachiman Shrine

Pacific Ocean

D1164556

SHINTO

KODANSHA INTERNATIONAL LTD.

Tokyo, New York and San Francisco

Stuart D. B. Picken

Introduction by Edwin O. Reischauer

SHINTO

Japan's Spiritual Roots

INTRODUCTION

It would be hard to imagine Japan without Shinto or Shinto anywhere but in Japan. The two of course are not synonymous. Japan is Shinto and a great deal more. But no element in Japanese culture has run so persistently through the whole history of the Japanese people from their earliest beginnings right up to the present day or so consistently colored their attitudes toward life and the world around them. Shinto has been an unchanging warp on which a rich and varied woof of other threads has been woven into the constantly changing patterns of Japanese civilization. These patterns can be brilliantly diverse and confusingly complex, but they are always subtly influenced by the constant, continuing threads of Shinto.

Our earliest knowledge of the Japanese shows Shinto to have been already at that time their religion, or rather their way of life. It was their way of understanding the natural world around them and their relationship to it and to one another. To them nature was beautiful and bountiful. They were awed by its fertility and wonder. They reveled in the richness and luxuriance of their island home. They felt a oneness with nature, seeking to merge with it rather than struggling to overcome it. That which was particularly wondrous, whether in nature or among people, they accepted as a superior object of worship, called *kami*. In fact, they traced their origin to the manifold *kami* of nature, as in the case of the imperial family, descended from the supreme Sun Goddess.

Worship of the *kami* and the ordering of human affairs were seen as part of the same activity, and were supervised by hereditary sacred leaders, in early times apparently feminine shamans. What we would call government and religion were one and the same. *Miya*, an early word for a Shinto shrine, became the word for a palace. *Matsuri*, the term for a Shinto festival, and the ancient word for government, *matsurigoto*, are both derived from the verb *matsuru*, "to worship."

Shinto in those early times had no clear philosophy or ethics, and it still does not today. It expressed an attitude of joyful acceptance of life and a feeling of closeness to nature. Life and death were seen as part of the normal processes of nature. There was no struggle between good and evil. The only concern was with ritual purity, perhaps originating in part from sanitary measures and certainly contributing to the Japanese love of bathing and their record of being undoubtedly the world's cleanest people throughout history. *Kami* were felt to be everywhere and were worshiped and prayed to as beneficent forces. These were the simple beliefs of Shinto in earliest times, and they remain the heart of Shinto today.

Our first clear picture of Shinto goes back more than a millennium and a half. The early Japanese histories, written down at a relatively early period in the eighth century, start with the mythology of Shinto and gradually develop from mythology into the story of the predominance of one family of tribal sacred leaders, which was to become the imperial line that still occupies the Japanese throne. Chinese records, derived from persons who had obviously visited the islands, date back some five centuries earlier but give a picture that fits in well with the Japanese accounts. Archaeology reinforces the story. There are the great tumuli of leaders of the future imperial line as well as of their rivals and many examples of what were to become the Three Imperial Regalia of the emperors—the sacred bronze mirror, representing their ancestress, the Sun Goddess; sacred curved "jewels" of still unknown significance; and the sacred sword.

Shinto in its early days had no name. It was simply a way of life. Only after a flood of influences from China had descended on Japan was a name needed to distinguish Shinto from Buddhism, Confucianism, and other ways of thought. The term *Shinto*, meaning "the way of the gods," is actually derived from two Chinese words.

The wave of culture from China started in full force in the sixth century and came at first largely by way of Korea. It seems surprising that Chinese civilization did not sweep Shinto completely away or swallow it whole by incorporating elements of it into its own religions, as Christianity did with the native cults of northern Europe. Japan was still a primitive land, while China had had a high civilization for at least two millennia and was just entering on an extended period of clear leadership among the civilizations of the world. But this did not happen, and Shinto lived on.

Chinese Confucianism brought with it a fully developed and extremely complex concept of political organization and a social and ethical system to match it. These the Japanese accepted with enthusiasm, devoting amazing effort and skill to transferring their loose association of tribelike *uji*, under the supreme Yamato group, into a bureaucratic, centralized "empire" on the Chinese model. The Chinese political system eroded over time in Japan until it consisted merely of meaningless titles and a theory of government, but Confucian ethics became steadily more ingrained in Japan, reaching their heyday from the seventeenth to the early nineteenth centuries under the rule of the Tokugawa shoguns. Though subsequently rejected as Japan's political philosophy and supplanted by Western political ideas and to some extent by ethical concepts derived from Christianity, Confucianism still remains a strong ethical foundation for contemporary Japan. And yet Shinto practices have persisted during all this time relatively unchanged; Shinto attitudes toward nature and life have retained their validity; and the sacred nature of the emperors as the chief performers of the Shinto cults has continued unchanged for almost a thousand years after the emperors lost their temporal power as Chinese-type rulers and more than a century after the Meiji Restoration of 1868 returned secular power to them in theory even if not in reality.

Buddhism, starting around the fifth century B.C. in India and developing into an extraordinarily diverse and complex religion over time as it spread from India to China and Korea, might more easily than Confucianism have swallowed Shinto whole. It did this to other religions elsewhere in Asia, and in Japan it soon developed the concept that Shinto beliefs and *kami* were simply the local manifestation of universal Buddhist principles and deities. This doctrine, elaborated by Buddhist monks of the Shingon sect, was known as *ryōbu* Shinto, or "Dual Shinto." It persisted through the whole premodern history of Japan, and the two religions became institutionally very much intertwined. It took forceful action by the Meiji government in the second half of the nineteenth century to pull them apart. And yet, throughout, Shinto retained its distinctiveness and strength. While Buddhism tended to lose its intellectual vigor in recent centuries, Shinto took on new life, contributing to the anti-Tokugawa movement which resulted in a new political beginning in 1868 under the unifying symbol of the imperial line. Shinto also spawned the bulk of the "new religions," such as Tenrikyō, which rose during the past century and a half to answer the spiritual needs of the common man in the changing environment of the modern world.

Perhaps Shinto has survived so strongly in Japan because it had its own secure niche in the Japanese way of life. Confucianism dealt with political organization, ethical precepts, and a rational view of the universe. Concepts derived from the West provided these same things for the modern Japanese. Buddhism was concerned with the relation of the individual soul to the limitless cosmos and the afterlife, stressing either escape from the unending cycle of painful existences through enlightenment or salvation by faith into paradise. Christianity, too, addressed these same problems. But Shinto was focused on adapting to life in this world and on a simple merging of man into the natural environment around him. There was room for all three levels of understanding. A person could be a Buddhist in his ideas about the other world, a Confucianist in his ideas about government and society, but at the same time a believer in the Shinto *kami* and the Shinto attitudes toward nature in his everyday life. This is the way it has been for most Japanese throughout history, and this is the way it still is for many today. They feel no sense of conflict between these different philosophies and religions. Each has its own place and its own validity.

Shinto pervades the sophisticated, highly developed society of contemporary Japan, but it remains very much what it was as we first know of it from history. Efforts to distort it into something else have always failed in the long run. The attempt to graft the political system of China onto archaic Shinto Japan faded, turning into the very different system of feudalism and finally into democracy, but the Shinto roots persisted with little change. Buddhism sought to incorporate Shinto into its all-embracing theology, but in the process was probably more influenced by Shinto than Shinto was by it. The nineteenth-century modernizers of Japan and the twentieth-century imperial expansionists both tried to shape Shinto to fit their needs, but they and their ideas have passed into history, while Shinto continues to be what it has always been, an unassertive but powerful current flowing below the surface turmoil of political and social change.

It is amazing how true Shinto remains to its early beginnings. The shrines of Shinto are to be found everywhere throughout the land—the great Ise Shrines of the Sun Goddess, unchanged from prehistoric times through continual faithful reproductions of their original form; the equally moving and magnificent shrine in Tokyo built in this century to the memory of Emperor Meiji; the village shrines dedicated to the progenitors of some long-vanished tribal *uji*; the shrines that celebrate the spirit of some great waterfall or mountain; the tiny boxlike shrines in front of gnarled old trees; the shrines tucked into tiny corners of the busy downtown sections of cities or placed on the roofs of many-storied buildings; and the *kamidana*, or "god shelves," for worship of the ancestors within private homes. The *kami* are still to be found everywhere throughout the islands of Japan, and Shinto ways still permeate life.

The *matsuri*, or Shinto festivals, with all their color and gay bustle, still loom large in rural life and have helped shape the historical parades and public festivities of urban Japan. Shinto lies behind most of the seasonal holidays, with their distinctive activities, special foods, traditional clothing, New Year calls, visits to shrines, remembrance of ancestors, and gathering of the family again at the old farm homestead or in the old home town. People still pray to the *kami* in private or at their local shrines, and Shinto rituals are still seen as appropriate for many occasions from marriages to the dedications of skyscrapers. Most important of all, people still maintain the original Shinto sense of closeness to nature and awe before its beauty, its creativeness, and its power. Yes, Shinto as it existed in primitive Japan is very much part of Japan as the nation is today and probably as it always will be.

Edwin O. Reischauer

PREFACE

Shinto is a less well known aspect of Japanese civilization than it might be. In the minds of some Westerners, it is still associated with militarism, while to others, especially scholars, an overwhelming majority of whom are interested in Buddhism, it is primitive and may be disregarded. Yet in recent years, a spate of books in Japanese and other languages has appeared drawing attention to various aspects of the uniqueness of the Japanese people. While some have touched on tendencies to ethnocentrism, one going so far as to coin the expression *Nipponkyō* ("religion of Japaneseness"), none have ventured to say much of anything about Shinto. But Shinto grew on Japanese soil whereas Buddhism was imported, and Shinto remains a religion peculiar to the Japanese people in a way that Buddhism is not. Therefore, in speaking of those aspects of Japanese culture that do not readily find parallels elsewhere, it seems necessary to make some observations about the manner in which Shinto has survived and the role it continues to play in Japanese self-understanding.

My own experiences as a parish minister in a rural community in Scotland with a Christian heritage about as old as the Grand Shrines of Ise suggested a ready-made analogy that I could use to indicate some of the important links between Shinto and the Japanese view of life as well as devise a basic framework for the arrangement of topics. Consequently, this book is not intended to be an exhaustive study of Shinto. It deals with it neither historically nor geographically in great detail. Rather, it seeks to convey the image of Shinto as the living spiritual roots of the Japanese people.

Roots are beneath the soil and are therefore hidden. Empirical studies tend to interpret in terms of what is obvious and accessible, frequently neglecting what seems to be present only indirectly. I may be accused of straining to force Buddhism and Shinto apart, since historically these two religions were closely related. Nevertheless, shrines are not temples, and at decisive points they distinguish themselves. My purpose has been to identify what is unmistakably Shinto and to detect some of its influences both in obvious and in somewhat less obvious places. But Shinto is doggedly elusive, and what has been attempted here is in a sense impossible, for it is counter to the spirit of a tradition that has consistently resisted imposed forms of rationalization. Yet the student of religion and society must try to offer some account of interesting phenomena as they present themselves to him.

What modest success this book may have achieved in fulfilling its goals is due to the efforts of a large number of people. The authorities of numerous shrines must be mentioned, particularly those at Ise Jingū, Meiji Jingū, and Mitsumine Jinja, for their kindness and personal assistance. Special thanks are due to Professor Motohiko Anzu of Kokugakuin University and the Japan Culture Institute, to Professor Toshihito Gamo, also of Kokugakuin University, who was a source of warm encouragement and indispensable assistance in checking the manuscript, and to Professor J. Edward Kidder Jr., whose resources as a historian are matched only by his kindness. Finally, sincere appreciation must be expressed to Professor Edwin O. Reischauer for graciously consenting to write the Introduction to this book.

1 The Floating Bridge of Heaven

In primeval ages, before the earth was formed, amorphous matter floated freely about like oil upon water. In time there arose in its midst a thing like a sprouting reedshoot, and from this a deity came forth of its own. And from this deity evolved a number of divine beings called *kami*, and foremost among these *kami* were two, Izanagi and Izanami. The other *kami* addressed them: "Set the world in order," and handed them a jeweled spear. Izanagi and Izanami stood then upon the Floating Bridge of Heaven, and plunged the jeweled spear down and sought for land, stirring the ocean. They pulled the spear up from the water, and brine dripped from its point, and where the brine fell into the sea it coagulated and became an island, Onogoro. Izanagi and Izanami descended. They dwelt upon the land. They built an eight-fathom palace and set up the Pillar of Heaven. "We have produced the great country of eight islands," said one to the other. "Here there are mountains, rivers, herbs, and trees. Why should we not now bring into being one to be lord of this universe?"

And so it was that they produced Amaterasu-ō-mi-Kami, the Sun Goddess.

—adapted from the *Nihon Shoki*
(Chronicles of Japan), I:3–11

In the Beginning

With beautiful and touching simplicity the ancient sacred writings of the Japanese people tell the story of creation from the moment when the universal mist spontaneously condenses to the final stage when the Japanese islands emerge. Two divine beings, Izanagi and Izanami, in innocence and purity enjoy the fruits of love and procreate the Japanese islands and a series of other divine beings, greatest among whom is the Sun Goddess. According to tradition it is her grandson who founds the imperial house of Japan after descending to earth by the same Floating Bridge of Heaven, which in the narrative seems to suggest the idea that heaven and earth are closely connected and that communion between the two is possible.

This mythology expresses some of the deepest feelings and thoughts of the religious tradition known to the West as Shinto, the spiritual roots of the Japanese people. Literally, *Shinto* means "the way of the *kami*." The Japanese word *kami* is usually translated into English by the term "god" or "spirit." But Japanese *kami* are not superhuman inhabitants of a distant heavenly realm. They are divine, yet close to the world of daily life. A *kami* is understood to mean anything that can inspire in human beings a feeling of awe, reverence, or mystery. When something or someone is said to possess *kami*-nature, it or he has a power to awaken within us a sense of beauty, joy, love of nature, or fascination with the universe. This is not primitive nature worship, but rather nature awakening in man a sense of the divine at the heart of the universe. It may be expressed as a love of nature, but also

神
KAMI

as a love of life itself and as a sense of reverence before life's power and vitality.

The image of nature developed by Shinto contrasts sharply with that of Western religions, particularly Christianity where the wilderness since medieval times has been a symbol of man's sinful nature uncontrolled by the discipline of religion and unredeemed by divine grace. This is perhaps the mark left by Western man's struggle with a hostile environment. The Hebrew people discovered God in the awesome silence and severity of the desert, where neither herb nor water may be found. Protestantism especially was tempered by the dreary coldness and long dark winters of Northern Europe, high levels of infant mortality, short life-expectancy, and endless cycles of disease and war. North American Christianity helped to tame wild and unknown frontiers and to build a new world.

NATURE

The Japanese in contrast consider themselves to be blessed by nature. Their islands are richly endowed with trees, water, and beautiful mountains. Nature is a mother's bosom to her children, the people, and nature is kind, with only the seasonal typhoon or fearful earth tremor to threaten disruption. There is in Shinto no equivalent to the Western philosophical distinction between man and nature drawn by the classical Greeks and given heightened moral significance by Christianity. So close, in fact, were the Japanese of old to nature and so indistinguishable was nature from man that when Japan began to import foreign concepts during the Meiji era, after the beginning of the modernization drive in 1868, a word had to be invented to express the idea contained in the English word "nature": *shizen*. Thoreau's life at Walden Pond, perhaps eccentric against the emerging urbanization of nineteenth-century New England, comes a little closer than most to a sympathetic feeling of harmony with nature similar to that which underlies Shinto.

In Japan, the four seasons of spring, summer, autumn, and winter—clearly distinguishable and of roughly equal length—continue to provide the framework for the Japanese view of life. Japanese schools and colleges matriculate in April, the springtime of the year, and have their commencement ceremonies in March, the close of winter. New employees enter companies on April 1, and new products, new television shows, and new serial stories in magazines appear with the breaking through of the spring flowers, the emergence of new life. Summer and autumn mark changes in the uniforms worn by policemen, schoolchildren, and company employees. These changeovers occur on official dates to mark the beginning of each new season. Department stores retail their merchandise strictly according to the rhythm of the four seasons; even in Tokyo, try as one might, it is almost impossible to buy winter gloves in July or air conditioners in December!

Alongside *kami* and nature in Shinto mythology is a third important concept. It is man, who appears not as a creature of the gods, but as a child born of the *kami*. In contrast to the myths of the Garden of Eden, from which man emerges corrupted and radically evil, in Japanese mythology human nature remains innocent, although people may perform actions unworthy of themselves. The *kami* know of sexuality and therefore anxiety about the more intimate aspects of life is not felt so intensely by the Japanese. Traditionally, mixed bathing in public baths was quite common, and is still found in some isolated inns and hot springs. There is no shame in being what is human. Rather it should be appreciated and fulfilled.

MAN

Life and Death

The Western response to this might well be that of a cynical realism pointing out that life, even for the Japanese, is not a perfumed garden. It has unpleasant and painful moments. People are born, they live, they often suffer—and they all die. How does Shinto face up to these harsh realities? One suggestion can be found in the poignant story of the death of Izanami, in some ways reminiscent of the Greek myth about Orpheus and his trip to Hades to rescue his beloved Eurydice. Among the *kami* to which

Izanami and Izanagi give birth is the fire *kami*. She was reportedly mischievous and her birth caused the death of Izanami.

Izanagi is beside himself with grief. His anguish grows and grows, and finally he makes the journey to the pass of Yomi-no-Kuni, the land of pollution to which the dead go. He asks Izanami to return. Unable to do this by herself, Izanami declares that she will seek permission, but that until permission has been received Izanagi should not look upon her. Izanagi cannot contain his feelings. After making and lighting a torch, he sees not the wife he remembered. He sees a decomposing corpse. So great is his shock and horror that he flees, pursued by some ugly female creatures, to the place where the land of the living meets the land of the dead.

One can hear in this incident echoes of past experience that gave rise to a taboo on touching dead bodies. As one source of the Japanese outlook on death, however, two important ideas seem to be implied. First, death as a process is considered irreversible. Death is a heartbreaking reality even for *kami*. Man also must accept it realistically. Second, while death is irreversible, it is not final, for just as heaven and earth are close, so too are the living and the dead. These ideas, as we shall see, give Japanese religious thought two distinctive characteristics that mark it off from religions such as Christianity, which think in precisely the opposite terms.

Purity and Impurity

The dead, according to the story, go to a land of pollution, a place of impurity rather than a hell reserved for moral offenders. Instead of the distinction between good and evil, the Japanese draw a distinction between what is pure and what is impure. The Japanese word *kegare* means defilement, pollution of purity, and is symbolized most dramatically by death. In Shinto, there is no hell, no last judgment, and no eternal torments reserved for the devil and his angels. The finality of death is faced realistically, since it ends in pollution and corruption. It is also faced confidently because the vital forces within life continue, and the spirits of the dead, once released from all physical limitations, become again part of the universal life-force.

The ancient Japanese, while perhaps poor in material culture, were rich in many kinds of spiritual awareness. Unselfconsciously they learned to commune with the universe they inhabited. The tradition of Shinto has continued to express this for them ever since. It is in this sense that Shinto underlies their culture and life. It is sometimes suggested that nowadays the Japanese are not very religious as a people. If being religious is defined as going to church every Sunday, they may not appear to be. However, there are around 100,000 Shinto shrines in Japan, and while some of them may seem neglected, none of them is in ruins.

The sea is recognized in Shinto mythology as a source of life. From its bounties the Japanese derived their traditional diet of seafood. Its *kami*-nature is revered in coastal fishing village festivals, and ritual bathing in the ocean for purification is still practiced. The freshness of the ocean in the light of the rising sun portrays two important Shinto values, brightness and purity, the ideals of a civilization in which the good and the beautiful are one.

Film catches the rushing torrent of the Oirase (*left*), a mountain stream in Aomori Prefecture, in a way that the eye of modern man cannot. As cave drawings have shown, and as modern photography has confirmed, the eye of primitive man was remarkably accurate in how it saw the subtle movements of all aspects of nature. Perhaps this is how the ancient Japanese saw their rivers and streams, as *nagare*, life that "flowed" in successive moments of endless renewal.

Wakayama Prefecture's Nachi Waterfall (*right*) is located in a region renowned for its breathtaking natural beauty. The surrounding mountains have long been regarded as a heavenly realm, and the sea, always a symbol of life, lies but a short distance away. Four hundred feet high, Nachi is the largest of a group of forty-eight falls in the vicinity, and it served as the principal object of devotion of a cult centered on the Kumano Nachi Grand Shrine, just up a hill from the base. The mysterious force and power of the waterfall identified it as a *kami* and encouraged the development of esoteric rituals in which its water is used. Waterfalls were particularly favored as places of meditation or purification by followers of Shinto-Buddhist mountain cults.

Legend says that Ama-no-Iwato, the Heavenly Rock Dwelling located at Takachiho in Kyushu, is the place into which the Sun Goddess retreated in indignation at the wild behavior of her disruptive brother, Susa-no-o-Mikoto. He committed such acts of impurity as breaking down the divisions between rice fields and filling up irrigation ditches, types of offenses purified in later ages by the rite of *ōbarae*. He also blew the roof off her boudoir and dropped in a piebald horse. The other *kami*, distressed that the Sun Goddess's disappearance had plunged the world into darkness, tried to lure her out by making noises. One of the *kami* succeeded by holding a mirror in front of the cave and declaring that another more beautiful *kami* existed. Out of curiosity the Sun Goddess emerged, and before she realized she had been tricked the clever *kami* placed a sacred rope over the entrance to prevent her return to the cave. She thereafter reassumed sovereignty of the Plain of High Heaven.

Mt. Fuji, or *Fuji-san* (*following page*), seen from Lake Ashino near Hakone in Kanagawa Prefecture, embodies the principle of the divine immanent in the world more than any symbol except the Sun Goddess herself. Some 12,360 feet in height and extinct since 1707, the near-perfect volcanic cone represents the ideal of the creative force that first emerged from the ocean. The custom of climbing Mt. Fuji, which became popular toward the end of the Edo period (1600–1868) and therefore predates the introduction of Western-style mountaineering, is derived from the ancient practice of climbing mountains for purity and protection against ill fortune.

2 The Flow of Life

Ema

"My child is handicapped and I become very tired. I ask for a life less filled with sadness and unhappiness. I pray for better fortune."

"I would like to find a nice home-loving girl to marry. I am fond of children and think I can be a good father. So I came here to pray. Please help me."

One moving experience possible for anyone who can read and speak a little Japanese is that of reading prayers like those written on the backs of *ema*, wooden prayer-tablets that are hung on trees at shrines or found in small buildings specially erected to house them. In the act of writing and offering these prayers, we can see another aspect of Shinto, as a way of calling on the *kami* directly at every stage of human life.

The assistance of guardian *kami* who specialize in granting this or that favor may be solicited in a formal way through prayer tablets like *ema* or through cultural practices and customs in which the *kami* are consulted and invoked. For individuals, the times at which these requests are made frequently correspond to the great moments of life. It is at such moments that the Japanese traditionally turn, not to the figure of the Buddha, himself an immigrant, but to the native *kami*, whose protective arms enfold even the Buddha.

Life Symbols

At the root of the Japanese feeling toward life is the concept of *nagare*, which means "flow," the flow of life. Unlike Western religions, where change and decay are related ideas, in Shinto, change and renewal are connected. Water in Japan, because it was pure, clear, and plentiful, suggested itself to the ancient Japanese as a metaphor for life: In the rivers and waterfalls that cascade in the mountains, there is a sense of endless change, renewal, purification, and freshness. So do the events of life flow in succession, and with the protective help of the *kami* they can be moments of endless renewal.

The rice fields of Nagano Prefecture in their autumn splendor serve as a reminder of the agricultural origins of Japan. The *dandanbatake*, terraced fields that follow the natural contours of the topography, are a distinctive feature of the landscape, the mark of a small-scale intensive rice culture. From this closeness to the land the rituals of Shinto developed. While Shinto may have begun in an agricultural society, many Shinto cults, such as those of Hachiman or Ise, were the product of a society that had at the same time achieved a considerable degree of social organization and political sophistication.

21

Ema (literally, "horse pictures") began as substitutes for the horses customarily offered to the *kami*, who were thought to use them for transport. The oldest *ema* were decorated with horses, but during the seventeenth and eighteenth centuries various stylizations developed, and now many different kinds of animals appear on them. Pictured at left and above is the *ema* repository of the Kitano Shrine in Kyoto. The *kami* receive many requests!

The ceremony of *jichinsai* is conducted to purify the site of a new building. Before the actual ground-breaking, a Shinto priest (*below left*) reads the *norito*, a liturgical formula, within a sacred area (the *himorogi*) bounded by rope on which strips of folded paper are hung as ceremonial offerings. Below, family and friends are enjoying a more than usually exciting *tatemae* ceremony as the framework of a new house goes up. The customs of the *tatemae* vary from district to district. The banner records the date of the event.

The social importance of marriage in Japan is suggested by the impressive rituals surrounding the traditional *kekkonshiki*, or wedding ceremony, here pictured at the Memorial Hall of the Meiji Shrine in Tokyo. The families of the bride and groom are to their respective sides, while the go-between couple sits behind. The red wedding kimono may cost two or three thousand dollars to rent for one day but is usually exchanged prior to the reception for a Western-style evening gown. Rice wine is being served by the *miko*, the priest's female assistant.

Seen wherever Shinto rituals take place, whether shrine, *himorogi*, or wedding hall, are a similar set of utensils to hold food offerings to the *kami*. Such offerings include rice, sakè, rice cakes, vegetables, fish, chicken, fruits, and candies. The green tree, in back, *sakaki* (*Cleyera ochnacea*), is sacred in Shinto.

Ideas, no matter how intellectually appealing, cannot be preserved unless they are represented symbolically. This is true in all cultures and civilizations. Consequently, ceremonies, rites of passage through the myriad phases of existence, emerge. The ceremonies of Shinto are similar to Christian and Jewish ritual in the way they encompass life with symbols that express something of its meaning and something of its mystery. From baptism to burial, the blessing of God is invoked throughout the life of the Christian. Shinto rituals, or life symbols, in their own way do the same for the Japanese, reflecting their belief in the unseen spiritual forces that influence the destiny of human beings.

Stages on Life's Way

In modern times, the flow of life might follow a course such as this: Akemi is twenty-three years old and graduated from her college in March of the previous year with a B.A. in English literature. She has been living at home since she graduated, attending classes in flower arrangement, cooking, and wearing the kimono. Her parents feel it is time for her to meet a suitable young man, but her opportunities are limited. There are no church choirs or Sunday meetings where young people with common interests and backgrounds can meet. She wonders what to do. Akira is twenty-eight years old, a graduate of a private university, and an employee of a large trading company based in the center of Tokyo. Akira's parents feel as Akemi's do, but his life as an office worker is intense, with little time left over to meet the kind of person he might be best suited to marry. Akemi goes for a day or two's trip and visits the Izumo Shrine where the guardian *kami* may help those in search of a partner. Some days later, a friend of the family calls and tells Akemi's parents about Akira. Photographs and personal histories are exchanged and a formal meeting takes place with the family friend as *nakōdo*, or go-between. All goes well, and one thing leads to another. Six months later Akira and Akemi are married. Was it luck? Was it the visit to the shrine?

The Wedding Ceremony

Whatever the true answer, the wedding ceremony takes place at a shrine. Akemi, if she follows the usual custom, wears the traditional kimono. Akira may wear either Western formal dress or the traditional Japanese *hakama*, a kind of pleated skirt. The ceremony is brief, simple, dignified, and impressive. The couple sit before the priest in the presence of family and close friends. Prayers are offered that the couple may be free of ill fortune and blessed by good things. As an act of purification, the priest waves his *haraigushi*, made from a sacred tree and with white linen cloth or paper streamers attached. All those present receive some sakè, Japanese rice wine, as a sharing of a holy feast with the protective *kami* who have been invoked.

The union of the couple will be prosperous provided they reverence the way of the *kami*. The Japanese believe strongly that while life may be full of difficulties, people should not be fatalistic. There is little room for pessimism in the social psychology of the Japanese people. Unhappy fate may be prevented if proper steps are taken to avoid impurity. Thus every important event in life is marked by a visit to the local or family shrine.

Ceremonies for a New Home

Akira and Akemi have set up home, perhaps in a small rented apartment or with their parents. If they are a little better off, and if Akira can get a loan from his company, they may able to purchase a small piece of land on which to build their own house. Once they have made arrangements to do so, they will be involved in a series of rituals and ceremonies which surround the erection of any new building or home and which express Shinto beliefs related to this event.

Once the area is marked off, the site is purified and the ground is broken in the ceremony called *jichinsai*, which seeks the cooperation and protection of the *kami*. When the basic framework of the house is completed, and the first vertical beam is raised to roof level, there is *tatemae* or *muneage-shiki*, the ceremony of raising the framework. Symbolic paper offerings called *gohei* are tied onto the top of the highest beam, and the carpenters receive some food and a bottle of sakè. These symbolize what was originally understood as an act of communion between man and *kami*. When their house is completed, Akira and Akemi will invite their friends and relations to a party to celebrate the great event.

What has been said here of the building of Akira and Akemi's house may be said also of public buildings, hotels, or large projects in civil engineering. *Jichinsai* will be performed by a Shinto priest and openings will be marked by a Shinto ceremony such as that held at the new Tokyo International Airport at Narita in 1978.

The First Born

Their house completed, Akira and Akemi have settled down to the routine of life together. As time passes, they decide that the birth of a child would complete their home. But no signs are in evidence. They might visit a doctor. They will probably also visit a shrine where the guardian *kami* helps such couples. Many such prayer tablets are seen in certain well-known shrines. The mood of the feelings in them is well captured in the prayers of Hannah (1 Samuel 1:1–2:11) who, infertile and unhappy, implored God to give her a son; her prayer was answered by the birth of Samuel, the great prophet of Israel.

In the fullness of time, a first child is born, and once again the shrine is visited in thanksgiving and celebration. Akemi goes there on the thirty-second day after birth because their child is a boy. Had it been a girl, the appropriate date would have been the thirty-third day. This ceremony is called *hatsu-miyamairi* ("first shrine visit") and through it the child becomes a parishioner. It has a similar status to the ritual of Christian baptism or Jewish circumcision, and it gives symbolic expression to the relationship between the child and the community of which he is newly a part.

Shichi-Go-San ("Seven-Five-Three")

In November of the year he becomes five, Akira and Akemi's child attends the shrine in the parish community to ask for the protection of the *ujigami*, the family *kami*, in the future. Girls of seven and three also attend, hence the name of the ceremony. In the past, November 15 was the festival day of parish shrines and people attended in kimono, making the event colorful and lively. But today's level of population mobility and the requirements of the job have combined to put many long miles between families and their home shrines. Domestic travel, increasingly expensive, has become for many a luxury reserved for special times of year. Further, many shrines that have no resident priest cannot attract a sufficient number of patrons to make *shichi-go-san* a local event equal in size to the spring and autumn festivals. Families now often prefer to make shorter journeys to some of the more famous shrines, such as the Meiji Shrine in Tokyo, which can provide spectacular settings for the celebration of the event.

University Entrance

Time passes. Akira and Akemi are beyond the first flush of youth and their son is approaching his college years. He regularly studies late into the evening, as does his sister, two years younger. Both of them, like all children in Japan, face what is usually called the "examination hell," the fiery ordeal of

The flow of life. A priest (*above left*) bows his head in thanks to the *kami* after a newborn child has been welcomed into the shrine's parish. Only the mother attends this *hatsu-miyamairi*, or "first shrine visit," possibly because of old ideas about ritual impurity after childbirth. Parents and their children (*left*) crowd the Meiji Shrine in Tokyo on *shichi-go-san*. Similarly, a group of happy twenty-year-olds (*above*) is celebrating coming of age in traditional style at the Meiji Shrine. Since they are dressed in kimono, these young women may find *seijin-no-hi* the perfect occasion for taking photographs to be circulated among eligible young bachelors. The kimono, once an everyday garment, is now seen mostly at ceremonial or formal occasions, or at places where traditional arts are practiced. It is lovely to look at but expensive to buy and impractical for modern life; many young women, just as they have given up the arranged marriage, now wear Western-style clothing exclusively.

Inside the house (*below*), respect is being paid at the Shinto *kamidana*, or *kami* shelf, below and to the right of which is the *butsudan*, the Buddhist family altar. The *kamidana* is for not only ancestral but also local and national protective *kami*, while the *butsudan* is used to express filial piety to family ancestors. Small shrines called *yashiki-gami* may be seen outside the old houses of influential families in town or country (*right*). Sometimes they are dedicated to family *kami*, and sometimes to a cult, like that of Inari as shown here.

competition leading to the national or top-ranking private universities, graduation from which will virtually guarantee a secure job and social status. Life for the Japanese child is a series of examination hurdles, all of which are important, and consequently, shrines are busy in the weeks preceding them. During February each year, the Yushima Tenjin Shrine in Tokyo, where the *kami* of learning is enshrined, is visited by over 2,000 people each day. If her son is aiming for an expensive private university Akemi may offer an *ema* for Akira's promotion, which would ease the financial burden of the tutors, books, after-school learning centers, and other related expenses of higher education. Japanese *kami* are well disposed toward worldly success, and they welcome it on the part of those who seek to achieve it.

Coming of Age

During the time that Akira and Akemi's children are in college, they will probably participate in *seijin-no-hi*, or "Adult Day." This national holiday, held on January 15 each year, marks the formal coming-of-age celebrations of the nation's twenty-year-olds. On this day these young adults are invited to their local town halls to receive an acknowledgment of the event, such as a fountain pen. Then, formally dressed or in kimono, they make their way in thanksgiving to a nearby shrine. While families may hold private celebrations, the national holiday serves as a reminder that those taking part, if they wish, have the right to vote and participate in the political life of the nation. A little of the ancient background of the custom was seen when the *enbi-no-ei*, or headdress of manhood, was bestowed upon Prince Hirō, the emperor's grandson, at an elaborate Shinto ceremony televised from the Imperial Palace on his twentieth birthday, February 24, 1980. Adult Day is one example of how Shinto has been absorbed into modern institutions, helping to integrate them into a fuller view of the flow of life.

Later Stages

At this point we may leave Akemi and Akira climbing toward the peak of their career and beginning to sense the lengthening shadows of age. As life draws to a close, there are shrines and temples which help people prepare for a peaceful death. On the whole, however, death has been consigned to Buddhism. Shinto, the religion of purity and brightness, is concerned more with life than with its end. But what happens when someone dies? The person becomes an ancestral *kami* who will be revered and consulted by his descendants in turn. Devotions within the home are centered on the *kamidana* ("the *kami* shelf") and the *butsudan*, the Buddhist home altar which, as will be shown later, is concerned in a most un-Buddhistic way with ancestor worship.

The rhythm of the Shinto view of life is described in the following report of a young Japanese student:

> The sun rises early, but cannot be seen for some time because of the walls of high buildings that surround the house. Yet an old woman rises with the sun. Climbing slowly out of her heavy bedding, she walks across the *tatami* floor to the window. Opening it, she faces the east and twice claps her hands loudly: "Please protect everyone today, too."
>
> The small cup of water and offering of rice are replaced with new ones on the white wood *kamidana* in the shape of a shrine, in the heart of which is a small mirror.
>
> Again she claps twice. Having thus satisfied her *kami*, she goes outside to sprinkle the front porch with water. By then, her daughter-in-law is up and together they begin setting breakfast.
>
> This is a typical morning for my eighty-year-old grandmother.

3 The Shinto Calendar

Matsuri

The central acts of worship in Shinto are associated with festivals (*matsuri*) that mark important times of year on the traditional Japanese calendar. Just as the flow of life of the individual may be under the protective wing of the *kami*, so too may that of the community. This protection is acknowledged, invoked, and appreciated in the *matsuri*.

Japanese festivals have developed over the centuries and embody the ancient Japanese view of man and nature in ritual form. Since they are occasions for reverence as well as rejoicing, they normally begin soberly enough but invariably take on an unrestrained carnival atmosphere. Turning the local shrine, which stands solemn and silent at other times, into a center of festivity takes only a few hours, but preparations for the event were probably carried out over a period of several weeks by townspeople working in their homes in their spare time.

Comparable to the American Thanksgiving or the harvest festivals of Europe is Japan's Autumn Festival, which can be seen in almost any country town. It begins with the priests offering the first fruits, including rice and sakè, to the *kami*. Then the people share in a kind of communion with their guardian *kami* by engaging in a great and lengthy celebration in the streets. Children in brightly colored kimonos, mothers carrying babies, and fathers and grandfathers in *yukata* robes jostle and mingle, stopping to buy a souvenir at a stall or a piece of grilled cuttlefish. The hot evening makes them thirsty, but there are many vendors selling cold drinks, and trade is brisk. The worshipers make their way toward the main shrine building, throw some money into the large wooden collection box in front, clap their hands twice to attract the *kami*'s attention, and stand in silent prayer. Then they go back to the stalls to meet their friends and share in the festival mood.

Somewhere, perhaps on a specially erected platform, will be the festival musicians. Some beat out rhythms on the *taiko* drums in a fervid frenzy while others provide the haunting music of the *fue*, the bamboo flute. They will provide the invigorating harmony until they are exhausted or so full of sakè that they can play no more! By that time, everyone will be going home to sleep. In large towns, not only are the shrine precincts filled with celebrants, but also the surrounding neighborhoods, and often great wagons are pulled through the streets. These huge floats provide ceremonial meetings between *kami* and townspeople, who exalt the *kami* throughout the town to receive their protection. Pulling these floats, a noisy but spectacular activity, especially when they are lit by paper lanterns, is the highlight of the festival.

In other districts, an *omikoshi*, a portable shrine, is carried vigorously by a large number of young men wearing half-length *happi* coats and twisted-cloth headbands. In small communities, the feeling is more intimate, with friends and neighbors meeting, happy that for one more year they have rice and vegetables. Other seasonal festivals follow this same pattern, in summer to seek protection for the crops against pestilence and insects, or in spring to ensure weather suitable for sowing.

A little of the variety and spectacle of Japan's shrine festivals is captured on these pages. The ancient Aoi Matsuri, held on May 15 at the Kamo shrines in Kyoto, is a sober nine-hour pageant honoring the harvest *kami*.

At the Kanda Festival in downtown Tokyo on May 15, an exuberant—and probably intoxicated—group of young men is carrying their local *kami* in an *omikoshi* portable shrine while moving in a ritual dance rhythm to the inspiring cry of *"Washoi! Washoi!"*

Merchants from all over Japan attend the Chichibu Night Festival in Saitama Prefecture on December 3, which celebrates the art of weaving. Large floats are hauled up a thirty-degree slope, and when they have reached the top the festival ends in a spectacular firework display.

Many festivals are small, quiet affairs. At the Iwashimizu Hachiman Shrine Festival in Kyoto (*above*), fish and birds are released into the water and air in a ritual that expresses a gentle feeling for life and nature. At the Kenketo Festival in Shiga Prefecture (*below*), the *kami* is carried ceremonially about in a leisurely procession.

At the Nachi Fire Festival in Waka-yama Prefecture on July 14, twelve *omikoshi* representing the imperial army "do battle" with a rival army (carrying pinewood torches) for three hours and then return victorious to the Nachi Grand Shrine up the hill. This festival is about a thousand years old.

Famous Festivals—Chokusai

In some parts of Japan, these spring, summer, and autumn festivals have become, because of their antiquity, size, or splendor, enormously popular tourist attractions. They also may be important because in times past they were first celebrated in the presence of a *chokushi*, or imperial messenger. They are called the *chokusai*, and are the highest-ranked festivals. Here, the first clear signs may be seen of the vital and continuing link between the imperial family and the Shinto tradition in which the place of the emperor remains to the present an enigmatic and unique one.

Each year, the Grand Shrines of Ise in Mie Prefecture celebrate the Toshigoi, or Spring Festival, and two autumn festivals, the Niiname-sai (November 23–24) at which the emperor offers the first fruits of the grain harvest, and the Kanname-sai (October 15–17) at which similar offerings are made in thanksgiving to the *kami*. These are perhaps the most prestigious of all festivals. As a spectacle, the Aoi Matsuri is renowned. On May 15, at the two Kamo shrines in Kyoto, prayers are offered for an abundant grain harvest. The procession starts from the old Imperial Palace and moves through the streets with ox-drawn carts, horses adorned with golden saddles, and everywhere decorated with wisteria. It is one of the three great festivals of Japan.

The second is the festival of the Kasuga Shrine in Nara, celebrated on March 13 and said to date from around the beginning of the twelfth century. The third great festival is the Iwashimizu Matsuri of the Iwashimizu Hachiman Shrine near Kyoto. At that festival, celebrated on September 15 around the time of the full moon, birds, fish, and other living creatures are released into the rivers and the skies. The festival has some Buddhist elements, but in its reverence for nature it is basically Shinto.

Obon

Every summer, the working people of the big cities exodus back to their home towns for the Bon Festival (Obon), celebrated to console the spirits of the dead. It is a Japanese equivalent of All Souls' Day, but with one marked difference. All Souls' Day in Europe was frequently met with apprehension if not fear because the dead were looked upon as marauders rather than friends. In Japan, when the spirits return to their former earthly homes, they are warmly welcomed. Family members provide a *mukaebi*, or "welcoming fire," at the entrance to the home and place offerings on the household altar. Two days after welcoming, the *okuribi*, or "sending-off fire," is lit to guide the spirits back to the graveyards. In some places, instead of the fire, lanterns are floated down a nearby river.

The Bon Festival, though clearly Buddhist in origin, was later strongly modified by Shinto ideas of the inspiration of the living by the spirits of those who have gone before. It is celebrated around July in some parts of Japan and in August in other parts, depending on whether the old Chinese calendar or the modern Western one is followed. Obon has considerable social and domestic importance, for it affords the living an opportunity to consult the dead on ventures such as marriage, a trip abroad, a change of job, or other important steps in which the cooperation of the ancestral *kami* is desirable. No small reason for its popularity, however, is the chance it provides the ordinary worker to escape the stifling summer heat of the city.

New Year

The most vigorously and busily celebrated of all Japan's festivals, the greatest family event of all, is New Year. The lively celebrations which usher in the New Year begin around the middle of December. Company employees have their *bōnenkai* (year-end parties), at which they "forget" the old year and prepare to welcome the new one. Once again, the city dwellers exodus back to the country, and seats on trains and planes become scarce. Around twelve million people mobilize for the journey, and they may be seen crowding railway stations, bus depots, and airports, carrying cases and paper bags full of gifts to take home. The journeys home begin around December 28, and for the next three days the routes from city to country are crammed with travelers.

At home, preparations have begun also. The women have started making the various New Year delicacies called *osechi-ryōri*. These consist of dried fish, *mochi* (a sticky rice cake), and other items, served colorfully but traditionally as cold dishes. The house is symbolically cleansed in a ceremony called *susuharai* ("soot and cobweb" cleaning) and the front of the house is decorated with *kadomatsu*, small pine trees joined to lengths of bamboo, the former serving as a symbol of prosperity because they are evergreens. Hung on the door is a *shimenawa*, a straw rope plaited to the left. From this there hangs a group of straw pendants with tufts in the sequence of three, five, and seven, the straw being alternated with paper *gohei*, symbolic offerings to the household *kami*.

Offerings are made to the ancestral *kami*, and these include *mochi* and some sakè. Different parts of Japan have different formalized styles of food for New Year, but the meaning and the purpose remain the same. Once these offerings have been made, the family sits' down to eat, drink, and relax.

New Year's Eve is enthusiastically awaited, and as soon as midnight comes, cries of *Akemashite omedetō gozaimasu!* ("Happy New Year") are exchanged. That morning or later in the day, the family will visit the local shrine for *hatsu-mōde*, the first visit of the New Year. Although temples are also frequented, shrines claim the bulk of the seventy million who pay the *hatsu-mōde* visit. Worshipers take offerings of money with them, and may be seen carrying home sacred arrows to destroy bad luck.

It is still customary for people to wear kimonos and for girls to play *hanetsuki*, a kind of battledore, in the garden or in the street on New Year's Day. The family may relax for the rest of the day or spend it in making preparations for going visiting or for receiving visitors over the next few days. Some like to climb mountains or go to suitable places to observe *hatsu-hi-no-de*, the first appearance of the sun on New Year's morning. In whatever manner, the arrival of the New Year is marked by special activities and events.

The shrine visit over, the rounds of visits ended, and the feeling of newness slightly gone, the family once again begins to think of the days of work ahead. Then come the dismantling of the symbols of festivity, the long tedious journeys back to the apartments and rented houses, and the less colorful workaday life. The holiday period is finally closed by the *shinnenkai* party that formally opens the New Year with the hope that it will be as happy and prosperous as, or better than, the year before. The decorations are burned around the fourteenth or fifteenth, and the New Year is now "this year."

There are many festivals in Japan, and many that pertain not to seasons but to places or phenomena such as fire or water. Some include elements of phallicism in which sexuality is used as a symbol of creativity. What is respected here is the life-force and its continual resistance to the threat of death. These rites may be traced to the story of the jeweled spear thrust into the sea from the Floating Bridge of Heaven and to Izanagi's affirmations about the power of life.

One lifetime's study could not exhaust the varieties and occasions of Japanese festivals nationwide. But wherever they are celebrated, and for whatever reason, they share the features of respectful acknowledgment of the *kami* and of participation by the people in acts of worship, celebration, solemnity, and festivity. In the beating of the *taiko* drums, the echo of the heartbeat of Shinto, indeed of Japanese culture itself, may be both heard and felt.

During the first days of the New Year, over sixty million people around Japan jostle their way to a shrine to worship and pray for good fortune and health in the coming months. Of that number, one million pay the *hatsu-mōde* visit at the Tsurugaoka Hachiman Shrine in Kamakura (*right*). The crowd is carefully monitored, and worshipers are urged to make their prayers as perfunctory as possible so as not to slow up traffic.

A child (*left*) welcomes her deceased ancestors back for the Bon Festival with a small bonfire. Later the ancestral spirits who have returned will be entertained by and asked to join in the *bon odori*, traditional dances that may wend their way through the streets or be held in the local schoolyard to accommodate the whole village. The lanterns in the Kyoto Higashiyama Otani Buddhist graveyard at night (*below*) show why the Bon Festival is sometimes referred to in English as the Festival of Lanterns. They are one of numerous Buddhist elements that characterize this summertime festival.

New Year in Japan presents numerous colorful sights. The outside of the house (*right*) is decorated with a *kadomatsu* (literally, "entrance pine"), the evergreen pine being a symbol of prosperity and good fortune. Displaying the national flag on holidays is still common on buses, highway tollgates, and public buildings, as well as private houses. Inside the house (*below*), holiday foods, *osechi-ryōri*, are on the table. A mother and daughter (*below right*) enjoy a game of *hanetsuki* in the quiet street outside their house. On the wooden bats are usually the faces of famous Kabuki characters. The shuttlecock is a feathered wooden ball.

4 The Sun Goddess and National Life

Ise Shrine

Of all the shrines in Japan, the Grand Shrines of Ise in Mie Prefecture are those most intimately connected with the destiny of the nation. The inner shrine is dedicated to the Sun Goddess, Amaterasu-ō-mi-Kami, the ancestral founding *kami* of the imperial family. The site has been a sacred place for more than 1,300 years, and in accordance with tradition the buildings have been carefully rebuilt every 20 years, but with no change in design or materials. The reconstruction is done entirely by Japanese joinery without using a single nail. On October 2 and 5, 1973, the present buildings were dedicated anew by the priests after the work had been completed by a total force of 200,000 craftsmen, carpenters, thatchers, and goldsmiths who made use of 13,600 Japanese cypress trees, 25,000 bundles of miscanthus, and 12,000 bamboo poles. The work took a total of 8 years and cost over U.S. $15 million collected from groups and individuals, rich and poor. Support also came from business organizations. In all, over $30 million was subscribed. The next scheduled rebuilding is in 1993.

When the shrines are rebuilt, the *kami* must be transferred from the old to the new buildings, and this takes place during the principal ceremony of the transference of the *yata-no-kagami*, the sacred mirror. To soothe the *kami* during the ceremony of transference and reenshrinement, an ancient form of court music called *gagaku* is played. The reconstruction of the shrine and transference of the *kami* is called *shiki-nen-sengū* and is carried out by the priests of Ise with the aid of dignitaries and representatives of the imperial family.

Amaterasu-ō-mi-Kami

The principal *kami*, the Sun Goddess, is acknowledged in the national flag, the *hi-no-maru*, or "circle of the sun," and Japanese still refer to their country as the "Land of the Rising Sun," although this title was in all probability conferred by the Chinese.

The Japanese reverence for the Sun Goddess differs very significantly from the worship of the sun found in other ancient cultures. There are no high stone altars on which human sacrifices were offered as in the empire of the Aztecs. Rather, the sun seems to symbolize light, and the most common representation of a *kami*, the object of worship in the inner sanctum of a shrine, is often a simple mirror. The mirror was chosen because it reflects light and therefore symbolizes brightness and purity. Frequently, the inner sanctum is empty. This suggests that a certain level of abstraction had been reached in Japanese religious thinking at an early stage.

According to one great scholar of the Japanese classics, Moto-ori Norinaga (1730-1801), the development of the concept of the Sun Goddess is the main theme of Japanese mythology as transmitted in the two ancient texts, the *Kojiki* (Record of Ancient Matters) and the *Nihon Shoki* (Chronicles of Japan). The early parts of both these texts give an account of the mythological beginnings of Japan. The myths themselves give the Sun Goddess a dual identity, first as the *kami* of the sun, and

36

second, as the ancestral *kami* of the imperial family. The symbolism is indeed powerful and carries within it somewhat obvious political implications: The greatest and most mysterious known force in the system of planets shares the same *kami* as the imperial family; the greatest reality visible in the heavens becomes the symbol of the greatest reality known and revered on earth. As a symbol of *kami*-nature in general, the Sun Goddess is more readily grasped than any other. Indeed, the Sun Goddess is a symbol of the nature which all *kami* share, and she is represented by her many descendants on earth. During the Meiji era the mythology was overtly politicized into what is known as State Shinto (*kokka* Shinto), and was used as the basis of an ideological cult of fanatic militarism. While that came to an end after World War II, there still remains a traditional relationship among the imperial family, the Sun Goddess, and national life.

National Occasions

Because of her prominent and preferred position, the Sun Goddess is formally consulted on all important occasions of imperial and national life. Visits to Ise are still regularly undertaken by members of the imperial family. These visits, however, are not always accompanied by wide publicity. They coincide with important events in the life of the imperial family and have been part of its annual schedule since the beginning of the Meiji era in the nineteenth century. In ancient times, however, when the emperor attended certain festivals at some sacred place, his pilgrimages might be joined by thousands of people in celebration and festivity.

In modern times, the prime minister and the cabinet usually visit Ise at New Year and after the inauguration of a new government or even after a reshuffling of the cabinet. Japan's modern constitution upholds the strict separation of church and state. A similar clause in the United States Constitution—and a precise, legalistic interpretation of it—may make it difficult for most Americans to get a feel for the intimate connection that exists in Japan between religion and national life. It is not quite the same as the English concept of state support for an established church which, among other factors, prompted the Pilgrim Fathers to set sail for the New World in search of a place where freedom of worship and conscience might be found. Rather, the Japanese people symbolically affirm their culture by recognizing the Sun Goddess as the spiritual mainstay of national life. The Japanese people have a very distinctive view of their islands, history, and language. They also have a special view of the country Japan, the constitution of its government, and its historical identity. Older scholars called this *kōkoku-shugi* ("imperial countryism"). In recent years some books have emphasized the Japanese tendency toward isolationism and Japan-centered thinking. While there may be a tendency to political isolationism in Japan, it would be unfair to ascribe this to the tendency of ethnocentrism in Shinto. Shinto was institutionalized and made the required faith of the people as part of the nineteenth-century political philosophy of the nation state. However, this was a political act and not the natural or spontaneous expression of religious belief. Shinto has since been unjustly condemned as militaristic and ideological, whereas in fact Shinto as well as other national traditions were the scapegoats for the real villain, the mentality of the Meiji Constitution which contained excessive quantities of the militaristic jingoism prevalent throughout the entire world of the nineteenth century.

The Imperial Family

What happened to the emperor in 1946 when he renounced his divine status as a fundamental part of the Occupation's abolition of State Shinto? Surprisingly little. In Japanese there is the word *ikigami*, which may be translated as "living human *kami*." It was used to refer to outstanding servants of the nation who might be enshrined and worshiped while still living. Imperial princes, national heroes, and

Spanning the Isuzu River, the Ujibashi bridge conveys the worshiper into the precincts of the Grand Shrines of Ise in Mie Prefecture. The architecture of the shrines, probably derived from storehouses of an earlier agricultural age, is admired for its simplicity and beauty. The layout of Ise is a little different from that of shrines in later ages: there are two compounds, the Naiku (which enshrines the Sun Goddess) and the Geku (dedicated to Toyuke-no-o-Kami, the *kami* of plentiful food), and each of the compounds has alternate east and west sites on which reconstruction takes place at twenty-year intervals. At left and below is the Naiku Shoden, the main building of the Naiku compound. It is part of the sixtieth reconstruction of 1973, and it occupies the compound's west site.

The aerial photograph above, taken in 1973, shows the new Naiku buildings (*lower part*) alongside the old 1953 buildings, which are in the process of being dismantled. The east site of the Naiku will remain empty until the 1993 reconstruction. The tradition of shrine reconstruction is said to have originated in the ancient custom of rebuilding shrines every year as an act of renewal. As populations became more stable and stylization increased, permanent shrine buildings came into use, and only periodic reconstructions were made to keep them in good condition. Today the Nara Kasuga Shrine is rebuilt every thirty years, the Kamo Mioya Shrine in Kyoto every fifty years, and the Nukisaki Shrine in Gumma Prefecture every thirteen years. Like Ise, the ceremony of *ōbarae* is of national importance. It is performed on the last days of June and December by imperial command. The priest (*right*) is reading the *norito*, which lists various kinds of offenses that anger the *kami*. The transgressions of the nation are purified by the tearing of the holy hemp.

some Shinto priests were thought of as *ikigami*, as of course was the emperor. But the emperor's divinity was clearly not the same as the divinity ascribed by Christians to Jesus of Nazareth, for its formal renunciation had little effect on the symbolic relationships that had endured for centuries among the Sun Goddess, the imperial family, and the nation. The emperor's action seems in retrospect less dramatic than it did at the time, as is emphasized in a document prepared by the Shinto Publications Committee for the Ninth International Congress for the History of Religions in 1958:

> Since the change was merely a change in outward treatment, it is only natural that, in the spiritual sense, the Shinto of the Imperial House and Shrine Shinto should still be considered orthodox. It is one of the noteworthy peculiarities of Shinto as a religion that, since these types of Shinto are not bound by dogmas and scriptures but preserve their life in traditional ritual form, in so long as there is no great impediment in the continuation of the religious rituals, the wounds inflicted by this change are not too deep.

The rituals have been preserved and the emperor continues to participate in the *kami*-nature of his ancestors and to function as a high priest, interceding and praying for the well-being of his people to the traditional maternal *kami* of the nation. Among the ceremonies for which he and his household are responsible is the great ceremony of *ōbarae*, which takes place twice a year at the Meiji Shrine on the last days of June and December. The *norito*, or liturgical formula spoken by order of the emperor during *ōbarae*, begins by summoning all the members of the imperial household along with the ministers of state; their participation indicates that the ceremony will purify and absolve every form of transgression found in the people. Two main types of transgression are identified. There are the "heavenly" ones, which include breaking down divisions between rice fields, filling up irrigation channels, and removing water pipes. The "earthly" offenses include the cutting of living or dead bodies, the incest of a man with his mother or daughter, certain diseases, bestialities, killing animals, and bewitchments. Altogether, they form a fascinating catalog of impurities that indicate something of the sensitivities and taboos of the agrarian rice culture that was ancient Japanese society. The method for removing these impurities is clearly specified in the *norito*:

> Whensoever they may be committed, let the Onakatomi in accordance with the custom of the heavenly place . . . cut off the top and bottom parts of the holy hemp and tear it into eight [meaning many] pieces.

After this act the torn pieces, believed to contain all the sins of the nation, are put into the Tama River west of Tokyo, whence they are carried to the sea.

National rituals anywhere are sure to be derided by some as meaningless gestures that have nothing to do with the real business of living. The millions of dollars spent on the Ise Shrines in 1973 could have been poured into parklands or recreation areas and made to serve the people in a more tangible way. Yet who can fix a value on tradition? Without the sense of continuity given to the nation by the Ise Shrines or by rituals like *ōbarae*—indeed by Shinto itself—the Japanese might have emerged from the period of modernization and then the postwar chaos with a much less firm conception of themselves and where they were heading. The energy they invest in the old traditions does indeed seem to serve them well.

5 Shrines and Kami

Kami-nature we have tried to identify as a general idea pervasive in Japanese culture. In individual shrines, as a result of associations that have developed over the years, particular *kami* or manifestations of *kami*-nature are enshrined and venerated. There are several kinds. The more abstract include, for example, creativity worshiped as growth, fertility, and productivity. Natural phenomena include wind, thunder, lightning, and rain. There are natural objects, such as the sun, sacred mountains, rivers, trees, and rocks that are regarded as *kami*. A fourth category includes certain animals, the dog for example, and particularly the fox. Finally, there are ancestral spirits; principal among this last group are those of the imperial family.

The many recognized manifestations of *kami*-nature are a result of Shinto's long evolution as a way of seeing and understanding the variety of phenomena that constitute the world of human experience. Individually, the *kami* have quite distinct functions, but in a unified sense they contribute to and co-operate with the creative processes at work in the world. Their special powers enable them to fulfill tasks at all levels of human life—individual, social, and national. Broadly speaking, a *kami* works in one of two ways.

The first is by means of a territorial coverage of the land. Eighty thousand shrines extending throughout the country are registered with the Jinja Honchō, the Voluntary Association of Shrines. Every citizen lives within the territorial bounds of a shrine and is protected by the *ujigami*, or family *kami*. Traditionally, people were protected by the *kami* exclusive to their family and area, but as families and communities expanded, the *kami* of the principal family in an area took on the role of protecting the entire community (whose livelihood may in any case have depended upon that family). Thus, the nuance of *ujiko*, or parishioner, while being concerned originally with family, came to refer to a community with the *ujigami* serving the people through a territorial "parish" ministry.

A second method is by having special areas of responsibility. These may be anything from protection against insects and blight in summer to (in more recent times) assistance in passing examinations, having children, painless childbirth, or the adequate supply of water. Such special ministrations and guardian relations are the basis of pilgrimages by those in need, or of the famous festivals described earlier in which the guardian *kami* are invoked for assistance or protection.

Originally, entire localities or even a whole mountain would be regarded as possessed of *kami*-nature. As people began to live around such places, or to wish for a talisman in the form of a shrine to protect them, the original areas began to diminish in size. Sometimes branch shrines were set up following the establishment of a new community. Traces of this are readily seen. The *torii* gateway marking the start of the road to Kamakura's Tsurugaoka Hachiman Shrine—among Japan's most popular shrines at New Year—is surrounded by buildings and buses and busy people, and the approach road runs through the heart of a shopping district. Over the years, land may have been sold, rented, or lent, but the position of the *torii* indicates what was once shrine territory. Tiny shrine

Located on the lower reaches of the Hino River in Shimane Prefecture, the Grand Shrine of Izumo (*right*) is the center of a cult that traces itself back to the mythological time of the *Nihon Shoki*. Shown in the winter scene is the famous, massive *shimenawa*, or sacred rope, that hangs in front of the worship hall. The shrine buildings of Izumo, like those of Ise, are in a very old style, and the main building, the *honden*, has been rebuilt twenty-five times in its long history, though not at regular intervals. But its towering 80-foot frame presents a startling contrast to Ise's much smaller scale. According to legend, the shrine originally stood 320 feet high, an indication that the majestic size of Izumo Shrine has always been one of its principal features.

Torii, formal entrances to shrine precincts, may vary in size from the huge ones found at Meiji Shrine to those that are too small for a person to pass through, and they may be located in the sea or in lakes as well as on land. The oldest *torii* probably consisted of either two posts with a sacred rope (*above*) or simply four pieces of undressed wood (*below*). Various styles developed, such as the *sannō torii* with its additional head pieces (*center right*). In the Heian period vermilion coloring was added under Chinese influence (*above right*), and later still, small *torii* standing in a line became popular, especially at Inari shrines (*below right*).

TORII STYLES

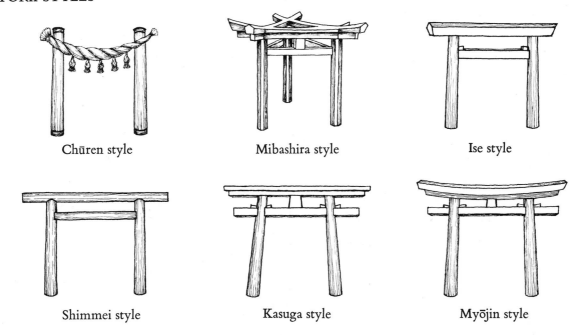

Chūren style   Mibashira style   Ise style

Shimmei style   Kasuga style   Myōjin style

compounds may be found in the central parts of large cities. In the Ginza or Akasaka district of Tokyo, for example, are many such shrines, some occupying no more than six or seven square yards of space. Small shrines may also be found inside the grounds of a company, or even on the roof of a building if space below is not available.

The manner of designing shrines has evolved over the centuries, from the ancient shrines of Ise to the relatively recent Meiji Shrine completed in 1920. The changes have tended to follow the prevailing aesthetic tastes of the periods in which the shrines were planned and erected. The shrines of the earliest styles made no use of color. However, the vermilion red *torii* and the more colorful buildings of the Heian period (794–1185) show the influence of Chinese tastes in design. Nevertheless, irrespective of era, all shrine structures share the essential feature of being made out of natural materials. Since the war, many Buddhist temples have been built out of reinforced concrete. Shrines in contrast continue to be made out of wood, although stone *torii* gateways are often seen.

Shrine Architecture

Shrine architecture is interesting because of its antiquity, although particular shrine buildings themselves may not be very old. There are altogether more than twenty distinct styles of shrine architecture. The names of these styles may be broadly classified into two types. One type may be labeled descriptive. There is *shimmei*, "divine brightness," of which the finest example is the Grand Shrines of Ise; they retain the love of purity of form that must have delighted the eyes of the ancient Japanese. Among others in this category that describe or express abstract ideas, most common are *nagare*, which means "flowing," typified by the Meiji Shrine, and *gongen*, meaning "incarnation," of which the best known is the colorful Tōshōgū at Nikkō. The second classification of names is made up of those borrowed from particular *kami*. The most famous of these is Hachiman, who after arising from obscure origins was at one point the *kami* that protected copper miners near Usa in Kyushu, Japan's southernmost island. Hachiman later became the greatest war *kami* in Japan, and is now enshrined in thousands of centers around the country. According to statistics, the most frequently encountered *kami* is Inari, who began as a harvest *kami* protecting rice but who during the Edo period (1600–

Inari style   Hachiman style   Tōhafū style

Sannō style   Ryōbu style   Miwa style

1868) inspired the popular cult of Inari, a *kami* who aided all classes in their search for material prosperity. There are about forty thousand Inari shrines throughout the country, distinguished particularly by their *torii* gateways and by the prominently displayed figures of the fox, long associated with the Inari cult.

The visitor may be confused by the enormous variety of architectural styles but with a little practice some basic differences may be detected. The two main features which offer clues to style are the design of the *torii* and the silhouettes or lines of the roofs of the main buildings. Generally, shrines face the east, but never the north, which is associated with death, or the west, which is considered unlucky.

Organization and Legal Status

How is shrine support organized nationally and locally? How are shrines financed and how do they stand with respect to the Japanese constitution?

In terms of local lay support, there are the *ujikokai*, the local shrine associations responsible for collecting subscriptions from every home in the *ujiko*, the people living under the protection of a particular *kami* in a particular area. A person who belongs to the *ujiko* is different from a *sūkeisha*, or worshiper, the status anyone may have if he wishes to pay homage at a shrine.

Especially in the Kansai area around Osaka, some shrines that are not served by resident priests are administered by a group of elders called the *miyaza*. Membership in the *miyaza* (or *ujikosōdai*) is still a coveted honor in most areas, for the group functions as the active link between the general population and the support required to maintain the shrines as living institutions within the community.

National supervision of shrines extends as far back as the eighth century when an office of shrine affairs called the *jingi-kan* was established having equal rank to the *dajō-kan*, the highest office of government at that time. Early in the Meiji era shrines were placed under direct government supervision. They remained there, with control passing through various government departments, until 1946 when State Shinto (*kokka* Shinto) was formally disestablished by order of the American Occupation authorities. With government control and supervision abolished, a national coordinating body was required to carry out certain necessary functions such as regulating worship and ceremonies and

Some of the best-known shrine styles are illustrated on these two pages. The austere *taisha* ("great shrine") style is thought to be the oldest type of shrine architecture and is represented by the Great Kumano Shrine (*above left*) located deep in the mountains of Wakayama Prefecture. As at Izumo and Ise, the roof of Kumano is characterized by protruding logs, vertical ones called *chigi* and horizontal ones called *katsuogi*. These decorations are peculiar to Japanese shrines, especially in the *shimmei* ("divine brightness") and *taisha* styles.

The Usa Hachiman Shrine (*above right*), located in Ōita Prefecture, is the principal shrine of the Hachiman cult. The style dates to around A.D. 765; the sweeping roofs, linked to the idea of reincarnation, seem to have been borrowed from Buddhist architecture. There are no *chigi* or *katsuogi*, and the way the two roofs are joined makes all Hachiman shrines easily identifiable.

SHRINE STYLES

Shimmei style

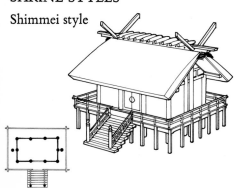

Taisha style

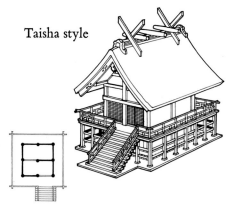

Nagare style

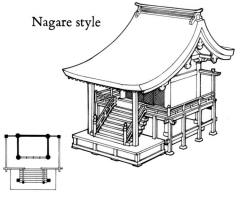

Unlike the Ise and Izumo cults, the Hachiman and Inari cults are not derived from the *Nihon Shoki* or *Kojiki* traditions but are more recent. Inari shrines are distinguished by the figure of the fox, messenger of the rice *kami*. The fox usually appears in pairs and frequently wears a red bib, for worshipers will place fried bean curd before him to gain his favor. At the large shrine-temple at Toyokawa City in Aichi Prefecture (*left*) is the distinctive figure of the fox, indicating the links that once existed between the Inari cult and Buddhism. As the small illustration at right shows, the shrine as a sacred place is unaffected by modern civilization. It is secure even in a concrete wilderness.

Hachiman style

Gongen style

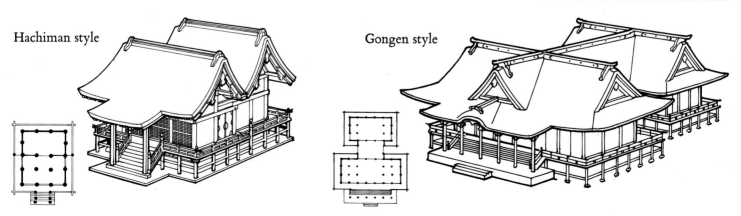

determining the qualifications of people to be priests. To this end, the Jinja Honchō, or Voluntary Association of Shrines, was organized in 1946.

The postwar constitution of Japan guarantees freedom of religion to all, and contains provisions that explicitly separate religious institutions and government functions. The shrines, thus removed from the possibility of politicization, occupy a generally uncontroversial place in national life, with one notable exception, namely that of the Yasukuni Shrine in Tokyo.

The Yasukuni Shrine was completed in its present form early in this century. It had been intended originally as the place of enshrinement of those who had given their lives in the service of the emperor during the struggles that led to the Meiji Restoration. As such it was founded in the second year of Meiji (1869) by imperial decree. Other spirits were added during subsequent troubles, and in 1879 its status was elevated by Emperor Meiji and it was given the name Yasukuni Jinja, "Shrine of the Peaceful Country." The dead of the Sino-Japanese and Russo-Japanese wars were added, and with this the image of Yasukuni emerged as the place of enshrinement of the Japanese war dead or of worthy people who had given special service to the nation—because of their efforts, the empire enjoyed peace and prosperity. The Yasukuni Shrine continued as a state shrine with the status of *bekkaku kampeisha* ("special government shrine"). Shrines for the war dead were usually called *shōkonsha*, and there were many in different parts of the country. Yasukuni now far outshadows any of them both in scale and significance.

A public debate was stirred up when, in 1979, the enshrinement of wartime and prewar military leaders including General Tōjō took place. While the act, in essence, was little more than an attempt to close out a painful chapter in the nation's history, people in Japan had a very mixed response to it, an indication that the status of the Yasukuni Shrine in the popular mind remains somewhat controversial and that it is not universally accepted as the symbol of the "peaceful country" envisaged by Emperor Meiji. Some war-bereaved families currently wish the shrine to be taken over by the state, while their opponents claim that this would be a violation of the 1946 constitutional separation of religion and politics. While it seems unlikely that the shrine will be taken over completely by the state in the immediately foreseeable future, no government body is likely to question the enshrinement of the late Prime Minister Hirota or even General Tōjō, since this too would be a violation of the religious freedom guaranteed by the constitution. Nevertheless, the stalemate has not affected the way Yasukuni is regarded by the average Japanese citizen, a manner roughly analogous to the way in which Americans view Arlington National Cemetery or the English view Westminster Abbey or the Cenotaph in Whitehall, which is associated with both national heroes and the war dead. Of course there are cultural differences to be taken into account—principally differences in the respective ways of viewing the relations between the living and the dead. But the idea of such memorials is essentially a product of the nineteenth century's romanticization of war.

From time to time, controversies are stirred up over the use of Shinto rites at groundbreaking and dedication ceremonies for public buildings. The claim is that through these rituals, for which priests are paid, governmental agencies are lending financial support and official recognition to a religion and are therefore in violation of the constitution. Occasionally cries go up that the revival of militarism is just around the corner. Doubtless there are some who would like to see this: Japan's ultra-rightwing has always been active. But it is hardly likely that the vast majority of the population could be enticed in that direction again, and the shrines are much happier being free to be places of religious activity and not symbols of a political system. At any rate, Shinto shrines and the *kami* to whom they are dedicated occupy a special place in Japanese thought and behavior. Irrespective of their legal status, their roles and functions will not change.

6 Shrine Life and Worship

Jinja

A shrine is a sacred place on which buildings of only natural materials are erected to enshrine a *kami*, who may subsequently be worshiped in accordance with traditional beliefs and rituals. A shrine is therefore quite different from a church, whose purpose is to provide a place for worship, teaching, and preaching. The European practice of naming churches or holy places after saints comes close. These names, however, are usually symbolic. The saint is not thought to be there. Even burial in a churchyard or inside a church is not equivalent to the practice of enshrinement in Japan.

A further point of contrast between the church and the shrine as places of religious activity concerns their location. While some churches such as in Bethlehem or Jerusalem are built on sacred spots or where miracles took place, generally speaking the site for a church may be selected in a quite arbitrary manner. The same may be said of a Buddhist temple. Shinto shrines, however, are located on sites chosen by the *kami*, that is to say, on sites that emanate a clear sense of the sacred. Whether by a tree, a rock, or a mountain, if a sense of reverence is engendered, it is natural for a *kami* to be identified and revered in such a place. It was with the same feeling that Jacob, moved by his sense of God's presence after his dream in which he saw a ladder stretching up to heaven, set up his stone pillow as an altar and poured oil on it, calling it Bethel, the House of God (Genesis 28). Actions like this are found frequently within the Old Testament. The sense of the presence of the divine as the basis of religion, described by the German scholar Rudolf Otto as *mysterium tremendum et fascinans*, the great mystery that draws us in fascination toward it, is the inspiration for the tradition of shrine building in Japan. In isolated places it is not uncommon to find *shimboku*, a tree regarded as sacred and marked by a thick rope tied around its trunk. Such trees were possibly places where it was thought *kami* had descended from the heavens. From the lingering sense of the holy in such spots, the idea of the more permanent shrine emerged.

The English word "shrine" is used to translate the Japanese word *jinja*, which literally means "*kami* place." Other names are used in Japanese, such as *jingū* or *miya*. These two terms are related, the suffix -*gū* being the same Sino-Japanese character as *miya* (宮), which means "palace." Shrines which are referred to as *jingū* have a connection with the imperial family, particularly Ise Jingū in Mie Prefecture and Meiji Jingū in Tokyo.

In ancient times, the shrine probably took the form of a *himorogi*, a sacred, unpolluted place bounded by rope and surrounded by evergreen plants and trees. For special purposes, *himorogi* are still set up as an area of purified floor covered by straw mats on which eight-legged tables are erected. A branch from a sacred tree is set up in the middle and paper streamers are strung on it. From these simple beginnings the modern shrine emerged as a colorful and busy place at certain seasonal festivals. Between these great events of the Shinto calendar there is a daily stream of worshipers whose distinctive ritual behavior is a living illustration of one aspect of Japanese religiosity.

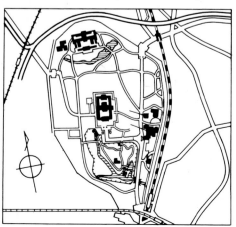

It is astonishing that the Meiji Shrine, surrounded by 120,000 trees, is located in the center of Tokyo and has connections with numerous enterprises nearby such as a baseball park and other sports and cultural facilities. It is not uncommon nowadays for shrines to support Boy Scout troops and other useful social services. Shrines may also serve as public parks, and they welcome children to play in the courtyard, old people to relax on seats in the shade, and lovers to stroll in their gardens.

The Meiji Shrine is one of the largest shrines in Japan. It is not as old as the Ise Shrines, but its location in the nation's capital and its dedication to the restored emperor and nominal leader of Japan's modernization drive have made it into a great institution. It is one of the most popular sites for performing the first shrine visit at New Year. Worshipers pack its grounds, inching slowly along the wide path that cuts through the forest. The great wooden *torii* (below) leads them to the *temizuya* (above), where they clean their hands and rinse out their mouths. In front of the main shrine building (*below right*) they toss coins and pray for prosperity and good fortune. Throughout the rest of the year, the Meiji Shrine displays the many different faces of Shinto. In the photo at right, for example, a dignified and austere group of Shinto priests is proceeding to a major festival at which an imperial messenger will be present. Altogether there are three ranks of festivals, and the priests' robes, headdresses, and shoes are different for each one.

Meiji Shrine

One of the most recently built shrines in Japan is the Meiji Shrine in Tokyo. It was completed in 1920 and then rebuilt in 1958 after destruction in an air raid during World War II. It enshrines the Emperor Meiji (1867–1912), the leader during the period of modernization, and Empress Shōken. Although built during the present century, the Meiji Shrine displays the classic beauty of the *nagare* style (see p. 46) and is picturesquely located in natural surroundings. Few visitors to Tokyo fail to see it. The quintessence of Shinto simplicity may be experienced there by anyone, yet in a setting that is close to the heart of a busy modern city.

At one corner of the broad Aoyama Avenue in downtown Tokyo, the *sandō*, or approach road, to Meiji Shrine begins and is marked by two huge stone lanterns. Known as Omote Sandō ("main approach road"), it runs downhill and again up a slight incline that takes one through the fashionable young section of Harajuku toward the main entrance. The *sandō* continues up to the *torii*, the unique gateway that marks the beginning of all shrine precincts. Meiji Shrine like many shrines in Japan has more than one *torii*. Other shrines may have two stone lions inside the *torii*; called *koma-inu*, their role seems artistic rather than symbolic.

The worshiper at Meiji Shrine follows the turns of the wide pathway toward the shrine's main buildings, a delightful walk on a sunny day. The main buildings are surrounded by a fence, outside of which to the right is the covered pavilion where priests purify themselves and to the left, the *temizuya*, the canopied area where worshipers symbolically purify themselves by washing their hands and mouths with water from a large stone trough.

Once past the *temizuya*, the worshiper proceeds toward the main buildings. Most shrines have three buildings, either under one or two roofs or, as in the case of Meiji Shrine, joined together by corridors. The three buildings are the *honden*, the *haiden*, and the *heiden*. The *honden*, or inner sanctum, is the area where the symbol, or *shintai*, of the enshrined *kami* resides. This part is strictly inaccessible to the public, and in the case of shrines with no resident priest, it is permanently locked or opened only by a priest at festival times. The *heiden* (or *norito-den*) is where the various religious ceremonies are performed. At the *haiden*, or worship hall, the worshiper offers his prayers. The prayer ritual is the same at every shrine: The worshiper first throws a cash offering into the box in front of the shrine. Then he claps twice, loudly so that the *kami* within will hear. Then, with his hands together, he bends at the waist and remains in silent prayer for as long as he feels is necessary. Finally he draws himself up smartly, again with his hands at his side, and quietly retreats.

After praying, a worshiper may request a talisman from a shrine or acquire some souvenirs of the visit if he does not belong to its locality. These are given by the shrine in return for a donation. Although nowadays it is customary to indicate prices, according to strict practice these items are not on sale. At Ise Shrine, the talisman, or *taima*, is made from the wood of the previously dismantled shrine buildings. Most shrines, too, provide private services, ranging from weddings to purification rituals for safety on a journey. On almost any day of the week, worshipers at the Meiji Shrine may see such special ceremonies being performed just inside the *haiden*.

Priests

Shrines are staffed by priests who qualify after undertaking a course of training at a recognized institution such as Kokugakuin University, founded as a center of Shinto studies early in the Meiji era. The chief priest of a shrine is called the *guji* and below him is the *gon-guji*. In large shrines, there are several ranks, such as *negi* (senior priest) and *gon-negi* (junior priest).

The Shinto priest is a distinctive figure in his white *shōzoku*, or formal robes, or in the dress appropriate to a season or festival. The term most widely used to refer to him is *shinshoku*. At ceremonies, *shinshoku* are assisted by *miko*, unmarried young women who are easily recognized by their white kimonos and full-length vermilion-colored divided skirts which are worn with white *tabi* (socks) and *zōri* (sandals). Priests are private citizens, and there are around 22,000 of them throughout Japan serving full-time at shrines; often those attached to small shrines also work as teachers or at other jobs in order to supplement their incomes.

Historically, the priesthood was confined to a limited number of aristocratic families who held responsibilities on a hereditary basis. During the years after the Meiji Restoration of 1868, priests were regarded as civil servants and the hereditary system was weakened. After 1945, it gradually began to return.

Purification

The concept necessary to understanding ceremonies at a shrine is that of purification. Just as the emperor performs the great *ōbarae* for the entire nation, so too individual priests perform ceremonies for the parishioners in general and for those requesting it for a special occasion. By these ceremonies, the *kami* are soothed and offensive impurities which distress them are removed. Three main methods of purification are employed.

The first and most common method is usually called *oharai*, which means removing polluting spirits and presences. There are many styles, but *oharai* is usually performed by a priest waving his *haraigushi* (described earlier on p. 24) from left to right and back again to the left. Also used is the *onusa*, a branch of a sacred tree or other evergreen to which linen cloths are attached. It is the ceremony of *oharai* that is performed in a shrine, or at the opening of a new building or public utility. One interesting special version of this is *yakubarai*, sometimes, but incorrectly, translated as "exorcism." In the West, exorcism implies removing a devil. In Shinto *yakubarai* means merely the calming of a troublesome *kami* who has been offended by some impurity. In June 1978, the residents of the Takashima-daira housing complex in Tokyo became concerned about the number of suicides in their community, particularly by jumping from the roofs of the buildings. After various forms of prevention and precaution had failed, Shinto priests were consulted, and the press later reported the ritual in which priests performed *yakubarai* to calm the *kami*. Other occasions on which *oharai* is received, in addition to those already noted, such as weddings, might be for purification and success of a candidate at the beginning of an election campaign, for safety on a journey, or for success in a contest. *Oharai* is not performed only for people or places. The illustration on page 54 shows a priest performing *oharai* on an automobile. This removes all impurities from the car, thus ensuring greater safety than would be possible if people were to ride in impure surroundings.

Oharai is also intended to show respect to any manifestations of divinity. The degree to which this respect may be expressed is most aptly demonstrated by the solitary *torii* that stands in the middle of the parking area in front of the Tokyo International Airport located to the south of the city at Haneda. The *torii* belongs to a shrine that was once inconveniently located where a parking lot for airport users was thought to be more necessary. The shrine was removed; but shortly after, a succession of accidents at the airport compelled planners to reconsider the hasty removal of the shrine and the possible offense it caused to the *kami*. Since restoration of the shrine might make the *kami* even more restive, a compromise was struck by replacing the *torii* alone in its original position; this now gives travelers the added feeling of security that they are, in arriving at the airport, reaching the security of a hallowed place.

Shinto showed its relevance in a world far removed from the simple devotion to nature of ancient

Worshipers stand under the 220-foot Shasui Waterfall in Ashigarakami County, Kanagawa Prefecture (*left*). This type of purification by water contains Shinto along with Buddhist elements such as the holding of prayer beads, the use of esoteric hand postures, and the recitation of *mantra*, or sacred songs derived from ancient Indian scriptures. Such rituals are ideally performed naked, either at the mouth of a river or under a waterfall. The order for washing the body is usually as follows: the mouth, face, private parts, chest and abdomen, feet and legs, shoulders and arms, back, chest and abdomen again, and finally over the entire body. The action is meant to be symbolic of an inner purification and pacification of the spirit. Bathing in the ocean is also done, and at some festivals the *omikoshi* is dipped in the ocean for purification. Sea water in fact has more power than fresh water because of the presence of salt, the most potent of all purifying materials. It is not only the body or the ritual instruments that demand purification. Below, a priest is performing *oharai* on an automobile, an indication that the *kami* are flexible enough to cooperate with man in his complex modern world.

Food may be taken outside to enjoy in the midst of nature, or nature may be brought inside to enhance the beauty of food. *Ohanami*, the party for viewing cherry blossoms, is unfailingly observed by the nation every year (*above*). The early spring weather forecasts always include details of the dates on which the blooms will appear, and frequently pictures of them are telecast as they open out, first in the warmer southern regions and later in the cooler areas of the north. At popular viewing areas throughout the country enormous traffic jams, sometimes twenty miles long, build up as the crowds make their way to catch a brief glimpse of the flowers or to find an open space to sit on while they sing, drink, and eat.

Indoors, the Shinto ideals of cleanness and beauty are expressed in the way the *sushi*-shop owner keeps his counter brightly polished as he serves up one of Japan's most popular foods (*right*). Many traditional-style Japanese restaurants have not only a *kamidana* but many other symbolic adornments derived from Shinto, such as *gohei*, *sakaki* branches, and piles of salt at the entryway.

days when, on July 16, 1969, the ceremony of *oharai* was performed at the United Nations Church Center on behalf of the Apollo 11 mission to the moon. The ceremony, performed by the ninety-sixth senior priest of the Tsubaki Grand Shrine, was utterly appropriate to the Shinto spirit, for the moon influences tides on earth and in Shinto mythology the moon itself is recognized as a *kami*, Tsukiyomi-no-Mikoto.

A second type of purification is *misogi*, more generally referred to as *kessai*, which means purification by water. After Izanagi's visit to the land of pollution, he bathed in a river, and ablution as a means of purification became a Japanese art. The bath, public and private, is a part of Japanese life in a way it is in few other cultures. Some mountain shrines have special facilities such as waterfalls for *misogi* while others use the open sea for ceremonial purification in salt water. The sprinking of water in the *genkan*, or entryway, of a Japanese house has its origin in this custom. Some shrines provide facilities for worshipers seeking purification by *misogi* at waterfalls. Priests and worshipers alike may be seen standing almost naked under the cascading icy waters of a mountain waterfall in the early morning, ritually purifying themselves and becoming fortified to fulfill their tasks in life.

Third, there is *imi* or avoidance. This is in contrast to the other two types of purification which entail the removal of uncleanness or impurity by an act of "purifying," actual or symbolic. *Imi* was particularly observed by priests, who were enjoined to avoid contact with sickness, death, or mourning prior to performing religious ceremonies. Traditionally, women, because of possible impurity through menstruation or childbirth, were not permitted into certain holy places. Not until 1868, for example, were women allowed to climb Mt. Fuji. In modern times, forms of *imi* that continue in a notable way are those related to death. The period of mourning after a funeral is called *imi*, because of its impurity. A recently bereaved person will not attend a wedding celebration. Nor at a wedding will the *imi-kotoba*, or forbidden words such as "cut," be heard. Of the three types of purification, *imi* seems most closely related to folk superstition.

Sense of Renewal

What do Japanese people feel when they visit shrines? A survey conducted around 1970 of people who visited shrines yielded the interesting information that sixty-six percent of the men and seventy-five percent of the women interviewed experienced what they called *aratamatta kimochi*, a feeling of inner renewal. Visiting the shrine seemed to reenergize their bodies and minds, which had become fatigued by physical and mental activity. More recent random investigations confirm these findings and suggest that the desire to experience a sense of renewal is a part of the daily religiosity of the Japanese people.

One evening, I was walking through one of Tokyo's less fashionable areas—a maze of bars, cheap eateries, and trysting spots—and happened to pass a small shrine. Wondering about it—and especially about who would ever visit it—I stepped through its small *torii* gateway to have a closer look. As I stood in the shadows I noticed a tired-looking and slightly inebriated businessman peering into the shrine compound from a side entrance. He paid me no attention as I watched him toss his cigarette into the street, straighten his posture, walk as best he could to the front of the main shrine building, and then, after throwing a coin and clapping his hands twice, bow smartly in silent prayer. He turned about and, upon leaving the shrine area through the main *torii* took out another cigarette and paused to light it before continuing on his way. Whether this man came to the shrine out of habit, was just passing through, or was on his way to some important, dangerous rendezvous I do not know. But my head was filled with thoughts for this book, and it seemed to me that he was definitely walking a bit more tall and steady when he left.

7 Mono no Aware

Mono no aware is an expression that describes the uniquely Japanese way of seeing the world and its beauty. It contains many nuances. Its use in literature and in human psychology implies a feeling of sadness, while with regard to beauty it has been variously translated as "aesthetic sensitivity," "sense of beauty," or "sense of the beautiful." It is not merely the ability to recognize beauty as such. Rather it should be taken to mean sensitivity toward the aesthetic and the emotional as a basis for looking at life. It is seeing with the heart into the natural beauty and goodness of all things.

The Western tradition inherited, from Plato, a bias against such an outlook on life. Plato in his youth considered that beauty might be a starting point for the good life but later came to mistrust completely all forms of representational art. In his great work *The Republic*, he banned artists and poets from the state. Within his soul there began the conflict between the artist and the scientist, the aesthete and the saint that later produced such polarities as romanticism and puritanism and such exaggerated personalities as Rousseau representing the one and Calvin the other.

Creativity

The strong emphasis upon the scientific at the expense of the aesthetic gave rise to the characteristically Western stress on the "cult of consciousness," which is seen in the need to formulate in exact verbal terms everything from the laws of nature to the principles of art appreciation. Western thinking in this respect appears to be based on three assumptions: first, that conscious states of mind are more important and influential than unconscious ones; second, that scientific rationality is the paradigm of all knowledge; and third, that aesthetic intuition is inferior to scientific understanding.

Each of these independently has been called into question in recent times. Freud and Jung showed in the early years of this century how the unconscious mind shapes behavior and decisions more than most people realized. Recent investigations into the nature of revolutionary scientific discoveries have suggested that truths are usually uncovered before proofs are devised for them. As for rationality being more important than intuition, the entire advertising industry, it might be pointed out, is based upon a profound appeal to the irrational side of human nature.

It may be that the aesthetic imagination plays a more decisive role in behavior than is often thought and that rationality is a special mood of the mind rather than its usual state. It is also probably true that there is more than one type of rationality. Philosophers and psychologists who are interested in creativity have argued that intuitive awareness plays a large part in the discovery of new truths, and the biography of Einstein well demonstrates this. The most effective stimulants to creative philosophical reflection seem to be anxiety or excitement. Neither is an ideal frame of mind in which to be calm and rational.

Moto-ori Norinaga (1730–1801), whose name has been mentioned earlier, made a similar point strongly and repeatedly in his writings. Shinto, he said, consistently refuses to rationalize or system-

57

Japanese gardens (*left*) were first based on Chinese models and later came to reflect Buddhist—especially Zen—ideals. But they clearly celebrate the special intimacy that Shinto fostered between man and nature throughout the centuries. Decorative stones in the garden are a good example. From earliest times the Japanese have regarded certain stones as *kami*, and today gardeners appraise a stone not just by its shape and color but by what they feel to be its "inner life." When a stone is aptly placed in the garden it is said to "live," and by this is meant that the stone's inner qualities are apparent as they radiate from within, providing a strain of permanence that counterpoints the garden's active growth and seasonal change.

Although Shinto ceremonies often include the offering of a *sakaki* branch to a *kami*, the Japanese art of flower arrangement, *ikebana* (*right*), is said to have originated from the seventh-century custom of offering flowers to the Buddha. But the art became stylized as it received inspiration from the Japanese aesthetic sensibility. Shinto ideals certainly lie behind *ikebana*'s goal of trying to reproduce nature by evoking its season and design. A typical arrangement presents the eye with a balanced form that is in three parts, one representing heaven, one earth, and one man. This corresponds to the framework of *kami*, nature, and man by which Shinto perceives the world. *Ikebana* has become a popular creative outlet for modern Japanese, and one reason for this may be that at a deep level, as one scholar suggests, it helps restore man's waning faith in the universe.

atize its insights. In his analysis of the ancient Japanese texts, he rejected what he called the *karabumigokoro*, the "spirit of Chinese writings." He was not objecting to the fact that there was Chinese influence on Japanese writing. After all, Japan had borrowed the Chinese writing system to articulate the Japanese language. Rather, he was protesting against the rationalist tendencies of neo-Confucian thought and Buddhistic analysis which had come to play an important part in regulating Japanese thought and life. He suggested that to adopt such an attitude of rationalization toward heaven and earth and their origin was to develop a mood of indifference toward the irrational, toward the transcendent and the mysterious that are beyond man. He regarded the ancient Japanese scriptures as a mirror in which *kami*-nature is reflected, and his work lay in exposing the nature of the suprarational absolute which he perceived through their mythology. One method of stimulating such spiritual awareness was by the cultivation of *mono no aware*.

Continuity

To appreciate the distinctive role of art and the aesthetic in Japanese life, it is helpful to contrast the role and form art takes in the Western world. For example, in the West, beauty is usually framed or made into a completed entity that is set up as an adornment to everyday life. Gardens and houses have forms imposed upon them for the convenience of their users or to produce patterns of color that please the designer. Paintings are hung on walls. In contrast to this, Japanese expressions of the aesthetic sense are based upon judicious rearrangements of life's ordinary or daily items into a form that shows their natural beauty and enhances their overall environment. There is less sense of imposed form than in Western art and consequently less sense of artificial delineation. There is, instead, emphasis upon continuity. The beauty taken in by the eye at any one time is only part of the total beauty. The world of Japanese beauty is the world of the incomplete and the encompassing where one element of form merges mistily and indistinguishably into the next.

The emphasis upon the continuity of form is very important, and is related to the concept of *nagare*, "flow," mentioned on page 21. The traditional Japanese house and garden illustrate this. Upon entering a room, the eye moves across the reed-matted *tatami* to the *tokonoma* alcove, which is usually adorned with a display of seasonally appropriate calligraphy and *ikebana*, a flower arrangement. But there is no "framedness" or sense of delineation since the eye glides slowly and smoothly from the *tokonoma* over the rest of the room toward the open rice-paper screens, across the narrow veranda of polished natural wood, and out into the garden where the highest levels of intimacy between man and nature are reached to create a setting of spontaneous beauty. Another way to express the contrast might be to say that the Western eye seems naturally to prefer the symmetrical while the Japanese eye more readily appreciates the asymmetrical. As to which is derived from which, philosophers perennially disagree. However, it is clear that the mind which thinks naturally in mathematical terms assumes that the asymmetrical is a deviation from the symmetrical, whereas the aesthetic mind might feel that the symmetrical is a special, accidental arrangement, a chance ordering in a world that is fundamentally asymmetrical.

The Japanese love for the asymmetrical seems to be derived from their distinctive way of experiencing and observing nature. The branches of trees grow as they will and flowers appear where the seeds happen to fall. Bushes and plants do not grow in straight lines, and stones and rocks do not have squared edges. Japanese artists have delighted in nature more exclusively than artists of other nations, and in a way that suggests a special intimacy. Their intuitive perception of motion (and as we shall see in the next chapter, sound also) has resulted in a style of reproduction that Western observers find difficult to understand. The downward-shutting movement of a bird's wings as it flies against the wind, difficult for the untrained eye to see, is, in the words of the great scholar Anesaki Masaharu, a theme "vividly treated in Japanese painting, but, curiously enough, never done by Western painters." Nature in art and the naturalness of art go together in Japan. Japanese art, in some ways, is an expression of the experience of nature.

It is sometimes argued that Japanese gardens require a lot of planning and that the forms are therefore not natural but imposed. However, that argument comes from a misunderstanding of what is meant by "harmony with nature." Nature here is not synonymous with "nature gone wild." Nature's own life forms must be sensitively understood, and man must study to discover how their optimum beauty might be expressed. Without guidance, nature can quickly become a jungle. The title of one of Norinaga's works, *The Spirit of Straightening*, suggests the idea of recognizing an already existing form and assisting or cooperating with nature to achieve the beauty of that form. And recognition of the form depends not upon mathematical symmetry, but upon *mono no aware*, seeing with the heart into the natural beauty of the world.

Art in Life

Some features of Shinto shrines were inevitably influenced by Chinese taste in colors and form. However, the oldest shrines at Ise and Izumo reflect the desire for purity and naturalness of form that lies at the heart of Japanese aesthetic sensitivity. This desire can be seen at work in other artistic areas of Japanese life. Zen Buddhism is usually given the most credit for the development of these. Doubtless Zen was a highly influential and a very noble patron of the arts. But the inspiration behind many arts belongs to Shinto as does the credit for the aesthetic transformation of Zen Buddhism in Japan.

One example of what is meant here might be found in the well-known tea ceremony. It is certainly true that the art of tea was developed within the context of the philosophy of Zen Buddhism. However, the ideals of cleanness and purity in the mind of its greatest master, Sen-no-Rikyū (1521–91), seem inspired at least in part by Shinto. So also does the attitude toward nature which he held. These are well illustrated by the story of what happened when he instructed one of his disciples to clean the tea garden. The disciple went out and washed the stones, the lanterns, and the steps several times, but each time he finished, he was ordered to repeat the process. Finally, the disciple in desperation appealed for an explanation as to why the garden was still not pure. The master went out and shook some autumn leaves from the tree and let them fall and be carried by the breeze where they would. "This," he declared, "is purity." Among the rituals of the tea ceremony, there is much washing involved in keeping all the utensils clean. This comes out of the need of *oharai*, or purification, as distinct from any doctrine in Buddhism, where the distinction between purity and impurity is of lesser importance.

Japanese forms of art and poetry, though they developed in Buddhist surroundings, owe a great deal to the ideals given life in Shinto. Japanese poetry emphasizes simplicity, brevity, and naturalness. *Haiku* poems use only seventeen syllables to offer a picture in words which the reader's imagination can readily grasp. Bashō (1644–94) was the great technician and perfected its form:

Kiyo taki ya	The pure waterfall!
nami ni chiri naki	Reflected in the crystal waves,
natsu no tsuki	The summer moon.

Japanese arts, particularly ink painting (*sumie*), are also exercises in the search for purity of form and elemental beauty. Japanese black-and-white ink painting is often deeply conceptual in content, but always very succinct in form. *Sumie*, like flower arrangement and poetry, is popular as a recreational pastime. It may be learned through a regular course of instruction. Even the young can learn

Pine Trees by Hasegawa Tōhaku (*left*), painted around 1600, is a particularly fine example of *sumie*, the art of ink painting. The world does not appear here as it is actually seen by the eye of man. Instead, quick bold lines and quiet modulations of black and gray—and even empty space itself—portray the essence of the forest. The observer of a *sumie* painting must have an acutely sensitive eye for natural forms. For it is in his emotions and imagination that he will find not just the actual physical object in the painting, but also what makes it unique in the world— its mood, its season, its way of exposing universal processes to yet another generation of life.

An actor prepares to make his entrance on the Nō stage (*right*), an immaculate eighteen-foot square of polished cypress wood. Nō—with its sonorous chanting and deliberate postures and dances—is unremittingly solemn drama. Yet its brilliant costumes and hauntingly expressive wooden masks give each performance an absorbing, if restrained, beauty. Curiously, this stately theater developed in the fourteenth century from earlier, almost vaudevillian entertainments of juggling and buffoonery presented at shrine and temple festivals. Painted on the back wall of every Nō stage is the Yōgō Pine of the Kasuga Shrine in Nara. Legend says that a *kami* once appeared before this tree in the guise of an old man and performed a dance, an event later reenacted each year when a villager would turn his body over to the gods and let them direct his movements. An actor today still considers himself "possessed" by his role, and before he goes on stage he will gaze intently at his mask as if to merge its spirit with his own. Shinto *kami* appear as characters in Nō plays, but their stories are laced with Buddhistic references to suffering and the transience of earthly life.

something of the art and practice it for its own sake and in this way experience the pleasure of creativity. Japan remains one of the few countries of the world where people can be found, in any significant numbers, who can write and illustrate their own poetry as a hobby, but who at other times are intensely preoccupied with the practical and often dull affairs of business and commerce. Such is the manner in which the sense of *mono no aware* imparted by Shinto comes as a source of renewal to the life of a modern civilization.

Visitors to Japan are frequently fascinated by the attention to detail exercised by the Japanese in the expression of the beautiful in the things of daily life. Trays of fish are garnished with tiny chrysanthemums, sandwiches by parsley, and *sushi* by seaweed. Toilets are decorated with potted plants, kitchens with fruit, and everywhere with flowers, sometimes even the dashboards of taxis. These are not empty gestures. They are expressions of the unconscious desire to create an environment in which the spirit of the beautiful is fostered to enrich life.

The relation between art and life in Japan is a mutual one which is difficult to find parallels for elsewhere. Lafcadio Hearn, in an essay on the Japanese smile, illustrates the point:

> I had turned aside to look at a statue of Jizō, before the entrance to a very small temple. The figure was that of a *kōzō*, an acolyte—a beautiful boy; and its smile was a bit of divine realism. As I stood gazing, a young lad, perhaps ten years old, ran up beside me, joined his little hands before the image, bowed his head and prayed for a moment in silence. He had just left some comrades, and the joy and glow of play were still upon his face; and his unconscious smile was so strangely like the smile of the child of stone that the boy seemed the twin brother of the god.

Which was the copy of which? The beautiful things in daily life are not simply ornaments of the moment but expressions of an age-old aesthetic understanding of the world and nature to be passed on again to future generations. The visual continuity of form that Hearn noticed is central to an understanding of how the Japanese can reshape the face of the present under the influence of the spirit of the past.

One of the highlights of the year for most Japanese is the *ohanami*, the cherry-blossom party. It is usually enjoyed in the daytime, but groups also go out in the evening and sit under the pale silvery moonlight, watching the cherry blossoms, drinking sakè, talking and singing. The cherry blossom which is universally associated with Japan is a little different from its cousin in the United States. It is single in its flower, and its color, due partly to the texture of Japanese soil, is more subdued than that of the rich blossoms found in North America. It blossoms quickly in the warmth of early April but, depending upon the weather, may last only a few days. Indeed, at the very moment it reaches full blossom, it begins to fall. This made it a popular flower of the *samurai* of old, whose ideal was to vanish from life, like the cherry blossom, at the peak of their glory. For centuries it has inspired Japanese art and music and has remained a symbol of the brevity of earthly beauty and the beauty of brevity.

Mono no aware is perfectly summed up in the famous short poem of Norinaga, composed at the age of sixty in 1790 and inscribed by him on a self-portrait. It provides a fitting close to this discussion.

Shikishima no	Should anyone ask about the
yamato gokoro o hito	spirit of Yamato (Japan)
towaba,	It is the wild cherry blossom
asahi no niou	Flowering
yamazakura bana	In the rising sun.

8 Shinto, Sport, and the Classic Arts

The importance of salt in Shinto as a symbol of purification is evident in many aspects of Japanese culture. For example, after attending a Buddhist funeral, mourners are given salt to sprinkle in their front entryways to purify their homes from the polluting influence of death. Stores still frequently pile salt outside for purification in the hope that it will pacify a *kami* that has become disturbed. During 1977's Japan Series, the baseball playoffs between the pennant winners of the Central and Pacific leagues, third base was the scene of several costly errors for one of the teams. What an American manager might have done to the third baseman may be left to the imagination. The Japanese manager, however, had a priest sprinkle salt on third base to prevent such recurrences, believing that the problem had other origins! Before the opening of the season, baseball teams often visit a famous shrine for *oharai*, purification from those polluting factors that might be a hindrance to success. If a professional baseball club behaves in such a way, it must be because these practices are thought to have some effect, at least on team morale.

Sumō

Sprinkling salt on third base was incidental to the baseball game. The sport in which salt appears explicity in the context of Shinto is the national and imperial sport of *sumō* wrestling. Indeed, all aspects of *sumō* are rooted in Shinto culture. *Sumō* history began at the shrines as one of the side entertainments provided during the great festivals. The original two tournaments were held in Tokyo at New Year and in May during the summer festival, but in addition there were numerous minor tournaments held around the country, such as at Yasukuni Shrine, coinciding with festivals in the spring and autumn. The number of major tournaments was increased to three in 1948 with the addition of the Osaka tournament. Tokyo received its third tournament in 1953. Fukuoka was added in 1957 and Nagoya in 1958 to make the present-day total of six, a heavy schedule of complicated organization and ceremony to carry out every two months.

During the tournaments, the matches of the top two divisions of wrestlers are telecast daily, and spectators can watch the rituals preceding each bout. The wrestlers enter the *dohyō*, the eighteen-foot-diameter straw-encircled ring, and are formally announced. After certain preliminary salutations across the ring, with hands open in promise of a clean fight, the wrestlers begin a series of movements from their corners to the center of the ring, where each one crouches behind a line and attempts to stare down his opponent and obtain a psychological advantage. On each trip from the corner to the middle, the wrestlers throw a handful of salt, sometimes a large and exaggerated amount, and sometimes just a few pinches. They crouch and face each other again and again until the prescribed four minutes has elapsed and the bout can begin. The winner is the one who forces his opponent to touch the ground inside the ring with any part of his body except his feet, or the ground outside the ring with any part of his body whatsoever. Simple enough, it seems, until the bouts which last a matter

The connection of Shinto and *sumō* can be seen as Takanohana (*left*), known throughout his career as the Prince of Sumō, tosses a handful of salt during the rituals prior to his bout. The *sumō* ring, from a distance and with the canopy in full view, retains its image as a sacred place. At the ceremonies before the tournament begins, the ring is purified, and in its center are buried offerings to the *kami*. Newly promoted *yokozuna* Kitanoumi (*above*) performs his *dezuiri* at the Meiji Shrine, Tokyo, in 1974 as the fifty-fifth Grand Champion in a line that stretches back to the seventeenth century. The feet stamping and hand clapping of this initiation rite is said to have begun when the *kami* made similar noisy gestures in an attempt to draw the sulking Sun Goddess out of the Heavenly Rock Dwelling (see pp. 16–17).

The martial art of *aikidō* (*left*) is a gentle, searching spiritual and physical training. It teaches the practitioner to develop his *ki* (the spirit's being in the world), to sense the *ki* of others, and to strive for natural movements that bring *ki*, mind, and body together. Although the art was established in this century, many of its ideals go back to early Shinto beliefs that man, nature, and the *kami* all exist in perfect balance with one another.

Yabusame (*above*) is an archery contest in which the competitors shoot arrows from a moving horse at targets set up in three consecutive locations. Like *sumō*, *yabusame* was originally associated with divination about the prospects of the harvest.

Bugaku (*right*) is one of Japan's oldest dance forms, but it is not a native art, having been imported from China and Korea between the sixth and eighth centuries. The elaborately carved, sometimes fearsome wooden masks are basically alien to native tastes and reflect their mainland origins. *Bugaku* was used for palace ceremonies in the Heian period, and though its development as an art stopped around this time, it is thought to have influenced the structure of the later Nō dramas. *Bugaku* performances were often held at shrines that were under the patronage of the aristocracy. Today, at the Kasuga Shrine in Nara and at the Itsukushima Shrine built over the waters of the Inland Sea, these ancient dances may still be seen. To the accompaniment of Japanese zithers, lutes, and flutes, the *bugaku* dancers move about in stately rhythms that honor and reaffirm the oldest values of the nation. Here at these performances, says art critic Noma Seiroku, "the music of earth rises into the realm of the gods."

seconds are observed on a video slow-motion replay and the styles of the seventy or more possible holds become distinguishable. *Sumō* is a highly sophisticated sport.

Sumō, entertaining as it is for both its pageantry and sporting excitement, has a background that is steeped in Shinto. The *dohyō* is sacred, and is consecrated by a ceremony of *oharai* before the tournament begins. Once the ring has been purified, no one except wrestlers or the referees (who for ceremonies connected to *sumō* function as Shinto priests) may stand upon it. When a stable (*sumōbeya*) for training wrestlers is set up or rebuilt, the initial ceremonies are conducted by priests. Each day the ring is prepared for training and cleaned up afterward according to prescribed Shinto rituals. Covering the *dohyō* during tournaments is a huge canopy designed like the roof of a shrine. Formerly, it was supported on four poles, which completed its image as a sacred place. These were removed in postwar years for a number of reasons, of which one was to afford a better view for television cameras. Because the older tournaments were staged to coincide with the summer and autumn shrine festivals, there is still the feeling among many of the tradition-minded residents of the older parts of Tokyo, where something of the old Edo spirit lingers, that the day's outing at the tournament is an event to be graced by the wearing of the kimono, dress appropriate to an occasion that takes place in the presence of the *kami*.

Every wrestler when he joins a stable has the dream of becoming a *yokozuna*, or Grand Champion, the highest rank in *sumō*. From *yokozuna*, he may retire, but may not be demoted. If a wrestler who holds the rank of *ōzeki*, next below *yokozuna*, performs consistently and wins about twelve or thirteen of his fifteen bouts in three or more successive tournaments, he is likely to be considered as a candidate for promotion to *yokozuna*. If the committee of the Sumo Association elects to promote him, he will perform his *dezuiri*, or first ceremony as a *yokozuna*, at the Meiji Shrine in Tokyo. The ritual involves the clapping of the hands and the stamping of the feet, both of religious significance. Thereafter, he performs the same ritual every day of the tournament prior to the start of bouts in the top division. The special costume he wears for this ritual includes a special colorful *mawashi*, a heavy silk body wrapping, with an apron front plus the heavy white rope called *tsuna*. The front of the *tsuna* is adorned with *gohei*, the symbolic paper offerings to the *kami* that may be seen hanging under the *torii* or in front of the *haiden* of shrines everywhere. He is accompanied by a swordbearer, the sword being an imperial symbol, and a herald.

The sport gained great momentum during the Edo period although its antiquity is claimed to be pre-Christian. The highest prize in each tournament is the Emperor's Cup, and one special tournament called *hōnō-zumō* is dedicated to the Meiji Shrine, which has had a close relationship to *sumō* ever since its completion in 1920. It is the Meiji Shrine authorities that issue formal documentation of a wrestler's status as a new *yokozuna*. In similar fashion, the athletes of ancient Greece dedicated their tournaments to the gods who lived on Mt. Olympus, thus beginning the ideal of the Olympic Games.

Sports and the Classic Arts

Not only *sumō* is rooted in Shinto but other sports are deeply connected there also. These were originally imperial entertainments and took place as "sideshows" at festivals attended by messengers from the emperor. There were two basic types of entertainment, one light-hearted and the other more serious. The former included nonsense and buffoonery of various kinds and was designed to entertain the population at large. But they were also performed to please the *kami* and sometimes contained stories or incidents from ancient mythology. In this way there was a transition to the latter type, the more serious stylized arts and skills that have been developed and polished over the centuries. Among the most famous of these is the *ashizoroe-shiki*, a horse-racing tournament that is held at the Kamo

Shrine in Kyoto on May 5 every year. *Kendō* (a form of swordsmanship), *aikidō* (a form of self-defense), and *yabusame* (archery) are all practiced at the great festivals today, just as medieval European tournaments presented the spectacle of knights jousting and showing off various other forms of the martial arts. However, there is one difference. The arts at the shrines were designed to entertain the *kami*, and consequently injury and death, both forms of pollution, were avoided. There is no record of the kind of violence at Western tournaments that sometimes led to knights being killed. The martial arts at shrines were simply demonstrations. They were not meant to be acts of mortal combat. But in other respects, such as their pageantry or their relation to seasonal or religious festivals, the parallels hold.

There is another parallel. In the West, the revival of drama in the sixteenth century had its origins in religious festivals at which the principal stories of the Christian tradition had to be enacted for the benefit of an illiterate populace. So, too, in Japan did the shrines make great contributions to the preservation of such arts as *kagura* (special sacred dances), *gagaku* (the ancient court music used in the transference of *kami* from one place to another), *bugaku* (a special form of classic dance-drama particularly famous at the Kasuga Shrine in Nara), and of course the highly sophisticated form of classic drama, Nō. Nō is a costumed, masked drama in which mythological themes are narrated and acted out, often in the presence of a *kami* figure, who usually explains the legend of the beginnings of a shrine or temple as an introduction to the play. On the occasion of special performances such as at New Year or at dedication or commemoration ceremonies, the play may be preceded by a sequence of dances called *okina*, whose beginnings were those of a religious ceremony performed by Shinto priests. Prior to *okina* being performed, all the actors take part in a ceremony of purification offstage. Unlike in other Nō plays, the principal actor puts on the special *okina* mask only after coming on stage and then removes it reverently and replaces it in its box before his exit.

Like *bugaku* and *gagaku*, Nō was originally performed outdoors on a low platform at shrines. Most major shrines that stage Nō performances now do so in theaters built expressly for that purpose. But these indoor stages are still built low and are separately roofed as a reminder of their original form. The outdoor performance points back to the Shinto association with nature and the appeal of a natural setting; similarly, the indoor Nō stage makes no use of scenery or stage props, except for, appropriately enough, a single painting of a pine tree on the back wall.

Music, such as that of the *shakuhachi*, a bamboo flute, is interesting to look at in this regard. The love of nature at the heart of Shinto has nurtured a "listening to nature" that in turn has imparted to Japanese music a distinctive tonal structure. Ethno-musicologists have commented upon this, and a more recent study by Sonoda Tadanobu of the Tokyo Medical-Dental College has suggested that there is evidence for the Japanese ear being more attuned to the sounds of nature than Western ears. He carries this to the point of saying that the differences can be used to show the structure of the Japanese brain is different from its Western counterpart in its arrangement of functions. While few might accept the entire theory, the doctor's observations seem to support the idea that the Japanese pattern of the apprehension of sounds derives from a long tradition of modeling speech and music in imitation of natural sounds.

At shrines up and down the country, the arts constituted part of the public celebrations of festivals, and in this way a precious part of the Japanese classical heritage was preserved and handed down from one generation to the next. As in Europe, both the sports and the arts gradually became independent of any religious identification and consequently secularized. But the deep links remain. Particularly in the case of *sumō* as a sport or *gagaku* as an art, without reference to their origins in the Shinto tradition they can only be enjoyed. They cannot be fully understood.

Intimations of mystery, mountain *kami*, a sacred animal, and the secret rites of a mountain cult in a silent and remote place high above the clouds can be felt by anyone who visits the Mitsumine Shrine in Saitama Prefecture (*above*). It is located on top of Mt. Mitsumine and is most conveniently reached nowadays by cable car. The Mitsumine wolf (referred to formally, however, as *o-inu-sama*, "honorable dog") is the center of a cult that dates back centuries, like the cult of the three Kumano shrines, to *sangaku shinkō*, a form of mountain asceticism. Pilgrims still travel to Mitsumine Shrine to practice discipline and seek purification in a setting of spectacular natural beauty.

In Wakayama Prefecture, on the south of the Kii Peninsula and near the mouth of the Kumano River, there are three famous shrines, the Hongū, Shingū, and Nachi. Their origins are linked to folk cults in ancient times, when the Kumano River region was thought to be the dwelling place of *kami*. From the Heian period on, these three great shrines were the centers of a cult that was a mixture of Shinto and Buddhism. In the tenth century, the imperial family began to make pilgrimages to the area, a round-trip of several hundred miles which was carried out with great pomp and circumstance. The *mandala* is an art form derived from Buddhism, and it was used in the Shinto-Buddhist cults to assist the mind in worship. Shown at left is the Kumano Nachi Shrine Pilgrimage Mandala, a Momoyama era (1568–1600) work. Measuring 5 feet high by 5.4 feet wide, it was painted on silk and is currently kept at the Tokei Shrine in Wakayama Prefecture. It shows the main shrine buildings and the related Buddhist temples with the great *torii* of the Nachi Shrine at the bottom. Nachi Waterfall (see p. 15) is on the right, and under it a wandering monk is being saved by a *kami*. Featured also is retired Emperor Goshirakawa (reigned 1072–86) worshiping in the shrine courtyard on one of his twenty-three pilgrimages. This *mandala* is an excellent example of how Shinto and Buddhism accommodated each other's legends, mythology, and symbolism as part of the Japanese transformation of Buddhism.

9 Shinto and Buddhism

Religious Identity

The image of Japan as a Buddhist country has distracted many casual observers from adequately appreciating the older roots of the Japanese tradition. The image exists for several obvious reasons. The most important of these perhaps is a result of the former custom of registering families at Buddhist temples, a practice which enabled the Edo government to keep close watch on the movements of all citizens. This practice seems to be responsible for the peculiar and interesting custom in Japan of drawing a distinction between family religion and personal religiosity. For example, if a Japanese is faced with the rather brusque-sounding Western question, "What is your religion?" he or she may respond as follows: "My family is officially Buddhist, but I am *mushūkyō* (no religion)." The public religious identity of the individual is understood to derive from that of the family, and on this basis it is claimed that, at least statistically, Japan is a Buddhist nation.

Given the above, however, it is possible for individuals to have personal religious experiences or to express religiosity in a manner quite inconsistent with the family tradition. But so strong is the family tradition that it is not uncommon for a person who was, for example, a devoted Christian to be buried by his family according to Buddhist rites even against the wishes he expressed during his lifetime. This may help explain why a nation that seems so easygoing on the matter of religious affiliation has proved so intransigent to the entreaties of the Christian missionary community over the years.

Buddhism

In Thailand, shaven-headed saffron-robed monks may be seen all over the countryside. Every male serves as a novice monk for at least six months of his life, including even the king. During that time, the monk refrains from meat, alcohol, and the company of women. But the Japanese *bōsan*, or Buddhist priest, has a quite different lifestyle. He may be seen at home, sitting with his wife and children in the residential part of the temple which he inherited from his father, eating fried shrimp and drinking beer or sakè. What explains the difference?

The kind of Buddhism found in Sri Lanka, Thailand, and Burma is called Hinayana ("the smaller vehicle"). Japanese Buddhism belongs to the tradition of Mahayana ("the greater vehicle"), which, as its name suggests, is broad and varied. Unlike Hinayana, preoccupied with problems about the purity of form and doctrine, Mahayana sought to expand and even cross-fertilize itself in new cultural settings. Its most dramatic and mysterious manifestation was the variety of Tantric Buddhism that developed in Tibet and became known to the world as Lamaism. Mahayana also developed in China, mingling with folk religion, Confucian social ethics, and the semimystical philosophy of Taoism. There it diversified into many forms.

Buddhism first made its appearance in Japan during the Asuka period (A.D. 552–645) according to ancient Japanese records. The ruler of a Korean state (Paekche), as a mark of tribute, presented statues of Buddha along with some sutras to the Japanese emperor. The figure most intimately associated with the early promotion of Buddhism in Japan is Shōtoku Taishi (570–622), regent to the Empress Suiko (594–628). (It is the face of Shōtoku Taishi that appears on the ¥10,000 banknote.) To the Japanese, Buddhism became known as *butsudō* ("the way of the Buddha"), in contrast to which the word *Shinto* ("the way of the *kami*") gradually came into use.

The Softening of Buddhist Doctrine

There are several distinct emphases in Buddhist philosophy that were affected by Japanese influence. Principally, its innate pessimism was modified. Buddhism may not be fatalistic, since release from the world process, *samsara*, is in principle possible by one of the many forms of enlightenment. But it is pessimistic, since the awesome power of the law of *karma* makes such release difficult to imagine. According to Hinayana Buddhism, a little of which came to Japan, it is understood that the world has no beginning and no end. People are endlessly reborn up or down the rank of beings depending upon the accumulated merit of their previous existences. The goal to be reached is that of eliminating suffering by eliminating desire in one's final rebirth. This leads to the state of *nirvana*, the cessation of all activity, which appears to mean that the only possible release from *karma* comes by achieving total extinction.

Such ideas seem hardly congenial to the social psychology of the Japanese people, and it is not surprising that the emphases which emerged in Japanese Buddhism tended more and more to simplify the process leading to enlightenment and to make enlightenment available to all. Buddhism in Japan lost some of its otherwordly qualities, becoming instead, like Shinto, a religion with an interest in this world. Traditional Buddhism stresses renunciation as a means of achieving enlightenment. The Japanese have never refused to accept rigorous pathways to achievement, or ones which call for even a large measure of self-denial. Self-denial and renunciation, however, are quite different. Renunciation of family and society implies principles of rejection and finality that run counter to the innate Japanese love of life and natural delight in its simple pleasures. Accordingly, the sterner demands of Buddhism became softened in various ways. One such way may be seen in the case of the development of the Amida cult. Amida Buddhism, or Pure Land Buddhism as it is sometimes called, had an interesting history, passing through various phases, including an association with esoteric cults, as in China, until a Japanese monk named Shinran (1173–1262) vigorously proclaimed the adequacy of belief in the one person, Amida the merciful. Entry into Amida's Pure Land, the Western Paradise, could be attained merely by reciting the formula *Namu Amida Butsu*, which is still used by the priests of the Jōdo Shin ("True Pure Land") denomination. It was Shinran who first abolished monasticism and permitted priests to marry, ideas diametrically opposed to the *raison d'être* of traditional Buddhism. It is significant that it is to temples of the Jōdo Shin sect that the majority of Japanese families turn for funeral rites.

The historical relationship between Shinto and Buddhism is as complex as it is fascinating. One outstanding feature that endures to the present is that Buddhism is the religion for death in the same way that Shinto is the religion for life. People are married at shrines, but buried at temples. *Sōsai*, or funerals according to Shinto rites, do take place, but only as frequently as marriages at Buddhist temples. Both are relatively unusual. It has been the vocation of the temples and their rituals to gild the mystery of death with a peculiarly Japanese interpretation of the Buddhist hereafter, in which elements of Shinto are clearly present. After the initial funeral ceremonies, the spirit of the deceased remains at home for forty-nine days, and on the forty-ninth day, the *shijūkunichi* ceremony takes place. The *butsudan*, or Buddhist home altar, is consecrated, if a new one is required, and the deceased, with a new posthumous name (*kaimyō*), is installed as an ancestral *kami*. At Obon, All Souls' Day, all the ancestral *kami* return and are welcomed in the manner related on page 32.

From what has been said, it will be clear that the basic outlook of Japanese religiosity contrasts sharply with those Western religions that have called for a form of commitment exclusive of possible commitment to any other modes of belief, even temporarily. It is best expressed by the formula "either-or." Japanese religiosity, fertilized as it is from more than one source, and in a spirit of tolerance, seems to believe that "what is true cannot be self-contradictory." Accordingly, Buddhism and Shinto not only have been able to divide the labors between them, but also have at times engaged in syncretism, the reconciliation of beliefs and rituals in the creation of a new religion.

During the Heian period (794–1185) there arose a form of religion that brought together the ancient tradition of *sangaku shinkō* ("the mountain-faith cult") and the esoteric tradition of Buddhism, a form of what is usually referred to by the general term Tantrism. Buddhist divinities came to be identified with Shinto *kami*. Something of the story is told through Japanese art in the Shinto mandala shown on page 70 that was devised to guide the mind, according to the Buddhist manner, on a pilgrimage. The objective of the cults that emerged was to assist individuals in developing supernatural powers through the discipline of mountain asceticism. One feature of this amalgam of Buddhism and Shinto, to which the general name *shugendō* has been given, is that shrine buildings came frequently to resemble temples, with the symbolism of Buddhism and Shinto becoming mixed. The Tōshōgū at Nikkō is an excellent example of a Shinto shrine that looks more like a Chinese Buddhist temple.

Shugendō was popular in the Edo period (1600–1868), although more as a religion of enchantment than as a mountain asceticism. It was formally abolished in the early years of the Meiji era (1868–1912) when Shinto and Buddhism were strictly separated and Shinto became an ideological tool in the hands of the new leadership. In the post–World War II period, *shugendō* has shown some slight signs of revival, and its ideas are certainly at work in some of the new religions that are designed to appeal to the common man by heightening the significance of his life.

On the whole, the influence of Shinto upon Buddhism probably has been wholesome rather than harmful. The Japanese aesthetic outlook transformed the more grotesque features of Buddhist art and iconography into benevolence and warmth just as the harsh lines of Buddhist doctrine were softened. For its part, Buddhism offered a metaphysical understanding of death, an area of thought absent from Shinto. However, even there, the ideal of "instant Buddhahood," a theme popular among Japanese Buddhists, seems the result of a non-Buddhist, humanistic influence. Perhaps most characteristic of all is the custom of *ohakamairi*, grave visiting. This is ostensibly a Buddhist custom of paying respect at the grave of deceased family members. But the Japanese carry rice cakes and fruit to the grave, indicative of a way of thinking that treats the dead as living, as *kami*. The dead in Japan are treated with respect and affection as part of an overall Japanese expression of gratitude to the past, and though this may be a custom of Buddhism in Japan, it is Japanese rather than Buddhist.

It is both easy and tempting to overstate the case for the influence of Shinto on Buddhism. At the very least, however, it can be said that, contrary to widespread popular conceptions, Buddhism in Japan owes a great deal to its relationship with Shinto. It may further be pointed out that while Buddhism underwent many transformations during that relationship, at the end of the process Shinto emerged once again, basically identifiable. A few branches may have been added to the tree, but the roots remained intact.

10 Shinto among the World's Faiths

People brought up under the influence of Christianity tend to view religion as something personal, based on individual faith and commitment. This is one aspect of religion, but by no means the only one. The view of the French philosopher and sociologist Emile Durkheim comes closer to expressing what Shinto has meant to the Japanese:

> Religion is first and foremost a system of ideas by means of which individuals can envisage the society of which they are members and the relations obscure yet intimate which they bear to it. That is the primordial task of a faith. And though it be metaphysical and symbolical, it is not therefore untrue. On the contrary, it conveys all that is essential in the relations it claims to portray.

As we have said, religious affiliation in Japan is considered essentially a matter of family tradition. The religion of the Old Testament was of this kind, as may be seen from Joshua's affirmation "as for me *and my house*, we will serve the Lord" (Joshua 24:15). The primary function of religion in Japan seems to be what Durkheim suggests: It supports the structure of community relations and promotes community values by expressing them through a set of symbols such as those expounded in the early chapters of this book. Myth and symbol need not be "untrue"; yet to fully appreciate the place of Shinto as a religion in Japan it is necessary to approach it in the first instance from a cultural point of view.

But can no account be given of Shinto beliefs or teachings? The desire for poetic and artistic forms of self-expression may have impeded the development in Japan of a tradition of philosophy similar to that of the Greek tradition. Not spelled out in dogmas, creeds, and theological propositions, the deepest insights of Shinto are instead preserved in aesthetic forms, and the descriptions already given here of Shinto practices come close to being an account of Shinto beliefs. Nevertheless, by reading the ancient Japanese mythology that the Shinto tradition reveres and by examining the attitudes that underlie important Shinto ceremonies and festivals, it is possible as an exercise in the philosophy of religion to infer a set of ideas which might be said to constitute the core of a Shinto "theology."

The sense of the mysterious at the heart of life, the desire to commune with it, and the willingness to express dependence upon it is the root from which all mythological expressions of religious experience spring. The way of the *kami* thus arose in the Japanese people of ancient times from their reverence for and preintellectual awareness of the structures of being that surrounded them. It has continued to the present in the form of an aesthetic awareness of life expressed in the creative, transforming genius at work within Japanese history.

The elements of this awareness are many, but four are supremely important if we are to appreciate the kind of influence that Shinto has had upon the Japanese way of thinking about life and experience.

Creativity

First, there is a profound understanding of creativity. This is implied in the Japanese mythological account of the universe. Japanese mythology as a whole is closer to pure unconscious intuition than to those types of mythology that contain elements of conscious reflection, or even explicit belief added as interpretation. The Hebrew use of the Babylonian epic in the creation story in the Book of Genesis is an example of the latter. In the Japanese myths, however, the knowledge that life has of itself seems to survive embodied within mankind's collective, unconscious memories. These creative forces are personified and made explicit. Everything animate or inanimate is the offspring of the *kami*, and man and nature share the common character of the "divine." This is an excellent illustration of what Teilhard de Chardin (1881–1955), the French Jesuit theologian and scientist, meant when he said that man was "evolution become conscious of itself."

The Greeks spoke of the world as created by a nameless First Cause. The Hebrews thought in terms of a Creator God. Christian theology elaborated upon both by defining one in terms of the other in teaching the doctrine of *creatio ex nihilo*. Modern science, intricate and abstract in its detail, and trusted by its devotees, seems to tower in superiority over the myths of antiquity that it claims to have superseded. Yet nearly all of the possible stages of modern cosmological theory from the big bang to the expanding universe have their counterpart in some type of ancient mythology. In the Japanese mythology presented in chapter 1, it is implied that the universe comes into being by condensing out of chaos. The first *kami* who emerged possessed the distinctive property of *musubi*, a word suggesting that self-generating creativity is responsible for all growth and development. The idea of spontaneity is used also to suggest the notion of a creative power within the universe that can and has sought self-expression. Within the sequence of creation, the gradual expansion of spontaneous creativity is suggested. First, the individual *kami*, Izanagi and Izanami, produce the Sun Goddess among other *kami*. The Japanese islands also appear. Then among the first generations of *kami* emerge two with seemingly quite "scientific" status. There is Takagi-no-Kami, meaning "high integrating *kami*," and Omoi-kane-no-Kami, meaning "inclusive *kami*, in whose thought the many are united."

Although there are many *kami*, they are not part of a polytheistic system. They are one in essence and manifest themselves in many forms in a world that is spontaneous, free, and creative. The varieties of manifestation of *kami*-nature imply an idea no more perplexing than the type of monotheism expressed in the Christian doctrine of the Holy Trinity. For both traditions there remains the philosophical enigma of how to consistently reconcile the insight of faith that divinity is "one" and united, with the observation of experience that the world of everyday life is "many" and varied rather than one.

The Beneficent World

A second "doctrine" of Shinto may be stated as a belief in the power, beauty, and goodness of life itself. After Izanagi flees from the decomposing form of his dead wife, Izanami, in the Land of Yomi, he meets her again at the Pass of Yomi, the place where the lands of the living and the dead meet. Izanami asks him why he has humiliated her by looking at her decomposing body, when she had expressly told him not to. He responds that so far as he is concerned, they are no longer man and wife, and he pronounces a decree of divorce. Izanami then threatens to kill one thousand people a day as a reprisal for his action. Izanagi declares that he will be able to ensure the birth of one-and-a-half times that number. Izanami returns to the land of the dead, and Izanagi continues his creative work.

From this story the point emerges that life is stronger than death. Izanami's threat to destroy one thousand people every day is met by Izanagi's firm response that he can create one-and-a-half times whatever she can kill. Life has a unique transcending power that enables it to survive and rise from the ashes of any disaster. Perhaps this is best illustrated by the progressive and energetic way in which the Japanese rebuilt their nation so quickly after 1945. It is the same spirit invoked over the centuries by past generations to assist them in rebuilding after earthquakes, fires, and typhoons which throughout the course of Japanese history have caused disaster and destruction.

Renewal is part of this outlook. Ancient Japanese frequently rebuilt their houses. Shrines almost everywhere are periodically reconstructed. One scholar has pointed out that if every shrine could be rebuilt every year, the ideal of renewal would be perfectly realized. This way of thinking contrasts sharply with the kind of ideal implied in the description of Rome as "the Eternal City" or the fascination in Europe and North America with ancient monuments built of stone or concrete to last forever. The Japanese have found ways of enabling things to endure by accurately transmitting form rather than trying to preserve content in an artifact built to stand to the end of time.

Shinto is frequently criticized for its lack of a formalized system of ethics. And it is often insisted that Shinto has but an inadequate and naive grasp of the problem of evil and suffering in the world as compared with "higher" religions like Christianity and Buddhism. One reason such criticisms arise is that there are hardly any Shinto documents or recorded sermons that address these issues. Could it be possible, then, that it is the Christians and the Buddhists who concentrate too much on evil and the negative aspects of human nature, while Shinto sees them as problems that man need not struggle with so fiercely?

Shinto does admit to evil in the world. What it refuses to do is accept that the world or the people in it are *inherently* evil. On this point, Shinto and Christianity are closer to each other than they are to Buddhism, whose sheer pessimism stresses that the process of life is inevitably characterized by suffering and death. For Buddhism, only the elimination of desire can lead to the possibility of release and enlightenment. For Christianity, however, evil and suffering are an intrusion into a world which God intended to be perfect. Sin is in no way inevitable. It can be forgiven and guilt can be expiated. In the Christian vision, after evil is finally banished from the earth there will arise a new heaven and a new earth, filled with righteousness.

For Shinto, this hoped-for world of the Christian is the world of everyday experience, the world in which the *kami* dwell. And it is a good world. The fierce *oni* creatures of folk cults are the closest Shinto comes to conjuring up devillike figures to explain human difficulties. Yet *oni* more resemble the first mischievous *kami*, Susa-no-o-Mikoto, whose actions so outraged the Sun Goddess that she took refuge in a cave. This is not diabolical evil but foolish roughhouse, and it suggests that in Shinto there is not evil in a sweeping, absolute sense, but simply perverseness of spirit. In this light, the role of purification as the basic form of Shinto ritual becomes clear. Whereas sin is forgiven in Christianity, in Shinto, through *oharai*, lost innocence is completely restored, man's spirit is balanced, and the world is made pure, returned to its original state.

Once the act of purification has taken place, such as that performed when a newborn baby visits a shrine for the first time, man need only follow his basic good inclinations. An elaborate body of ethics and rules of behavior is obviously not necessary when everyone has it naturally within him to do the right thing. In *The Spirit of Straightening*, Norinaga states the essence of the Shinto view that a moral sense is a natural property of human beings:

> Human beings were produced by the great spirit of the two creative *kami*. They are endowed quite naturally with the knowledge of what they should do and what they should avoid doing. It is unnecessary to trouble their thinking with moral value systems. If a system of

morals were necessary, human beings would be inferior to animals, who also have a natural knowledge of what they should do, only not to the same extent.

Shinto therefore emphasizes *makoto*, the virtuous ideal of sincerity, the sense of man being most truly and humanly what he is as a response to his awareness of the *kami* that surround him. Expressions such as *akaki kokoro* (literally, "bright shining heart") or *kiyoki kokoro* ("pure heart") convey the ideal in vivid metaphors. In Shinto, the highest appeal is always directed to one's better self.

Too often, morbid preoccupation with the horror and suffering brought about by history's Hitlers and Idi Amins, or with the meanness of our neighbors, leads us to reject the world and leave it to its evil. The Danish philosopher Kierkegaard broke off with his fiancée to symbolize how he had turned his back on the world, declaring, "Everyone should be chary about having to do with 'the others,' and should essentially speak only with God and with himself." Such an attitude is more appropriate to Buddhism than Christianity. Shinto's emphasis upon man most fully expressing his humanity in relation to nature and within the framework of social relations leads him into active participation in the world and is very close to the spirit of the Biblical metaphor that man was created as a steward of God's earth. There is in Shinto as in Christianity a consistent refusal to deny or reject the world as being in any sense evil or unreal. For both religions, whatever other differences divide them, the world of nature and society is too precious and too good to be surrendered to a demon or passed off as but another human illusion.

"Brightness" is a word that effectively sums up Shinto's perception of life, society, and nature. In one well-known analogy, brightness suggests the essential human spirit by saying that it is like a mirror free from dust and able to reflect its natural brilliance. Brightness thus suggests the absence of impurity; appropriately, the Sun Goddess—the supreme *kami*—is the brightest figure in the heavens. Traditionally, shrines are located in bright, sunny areas. A more recent expression of the Japanese people's love for brightness may be seen in their preference for eating in well-lit surroundings. There are in modern Japan, of course, many Western-style restaurants that are lit by candles and serenaded by soft music. But the classic Japanese restaurant is brightly lit, partly because food in Japan is to be tasted with the eye as well as the palate, but also because brightness is another natural quality of life, like cleanness, respected for its own sake.

Within Japanese society, the idea of goodness as a natural property of man and the world has played an important role in molding the Japanese character and in making possible a society based on co-operation, harmony, and trust. Whether or not Shinto alone—that "amoral" religion—is responsible might be debated, but the streets of Japanese cities are still safe, even for children and women who don't go to church.

Pragmatism

Implicit in the Shinto rituals that accept and purify both man and the world is an outlook that has been translated into a pragmatic philosophy of adjustment to change. This third Shinto "doctrine" has enabled the Japanese over the centuries to absorb the best of the great world cultures they have encountered without at the same time being absorbed by them. Japan has borrowed from Asia, especially China, from Europe, and from the United States. But it would be a mistake to consider these borrowings as the diminution of what is Japanese. They simply reflect the ability to absorb and respond to change as far as survival and success demand.

Japan virtually sealed itself off from the rest of the world in the seventeenth century. Yet in the nineteenth century, after some two hundred and fifty years of isolation, it was able to send emissaries abroad to discover and bring back the powerful secrets of Western civilization. Not only were the secrets brought back, but within less than a generation, Japan had employed them, and by the early twentieth century had become an important member of the council of nations. Of course, the impulse to modernization was stimulated by the experience of other Asian nations. Recognizing the threat of colonial domination, Japan chose to sacrifice some aspects of the past in the interest of the future.

Other nations exposed to foreign influence for longer periods of time today lag far behind Japan in modernization, political integration, and socioeconomic development. One crucial difference between these nations and Japan may have been the world view fostered by Shinto. In Shinto, the Meiji government found ready-to-hand political symbols to suggest that modernization was in fact a process of restoration of imperial power and not a revolution. The transference of power to the new leadership was consequently fairly smooth. Shinto also provided a measure of continuity even while the face of society was being "disfigured" by locomotives, industry, and foreign styles of dress. In the midst of change the old life symbols discussed in chapter 2 were able to encompass new styles of life and thought. In the sacred garden of the Heian Shrine in Kyoto is the anomalous sight of the city's first streetcar, a monument to modernization and a token of the pragmatic ease with which Shinto can reconcile new with old.

The recent postwar reconstruction was also a response to outside pressure. And it was certainly fueled by foreign aid. But it was effected as quickly as it was because the Japanese people themselves saw the need for it. The new society they have built, though superficially "Western," reflects values older than any bullet train or pocket calculator.

Universalism

The fourth, and from the point of view of the other great religions of the world a very important "doctrine" of Shinto, is its universalism, expressed as a desire to absorb and reconcile all within itself. When Buddhism first came to Japan there was not, as there is not yet, a formal body of Shinto doctrine. However, those aspects of the new faith that proved inconsistent with the aesthetic world view of the Japanese were gradually transformed. Some of these have been mentioned already. The ability to see *kami*-nature in Buddhas, or the reverse if need arise, has enabled Shinto to enter into a unique relationship with whatever it encounters. For this, it has been criticized as having no character. Nothing could be further from the truth. Shinto has never wielded the sharp sword of rejection, but rather with a spirit of gentleness has welcomed and shared in the contribution to be made by any faith toward the well-being of the children of the Sun Goddess.

Shinto is therefore neither unable nor unwilling to communicate or mediate between religions, or even cooperate with them. As a token of this, joint acts of worship have been held in Japan and in the United States involving Christian clergy and Shinto priests. Religious purists might feel disconcerted, but what is inherently wrong in people of radically different faiths seeking to express common hopes side by side in each other's places of worship? The more frequently such exchanges take place, the less alien the faiths become to each other. Shinto is the unique national faith of the Japanese people. It nevertheless possesses elements of a universal belief that may be shared by anyone. In an age of the meeting of world cultures, it is surely an important step forward to recognize that the uniqueness of one's own faith need not make it absolute or exclusive. It is significant that the first faltering steps forward have been taken. Perhaps they may lead to a gradual reconciliation of different perceptions of the divine and to a greater effort to achieve those conditions for which all true religions long, the peace and well-being of man and the world in which he dwells.

SELECTED GLOSSARY

Amaterasu-ō-mi-Kami: the Sun Goddess; according to ancient records, the founder of the imperial line

butsudan: the Buddhist household altar used to worship family ancestors

ema: wooden prayer tablets that worshipers post at shrines to seek the cooperation of kami in marriage, health, examinations, etc.

gohei: folded white paper or cloth pendants hung as symbolic offerings to the kami

haiden: the shrine building where the worshiper offers his prayers

haraigushi: the sacred wand waved back and forth by the Shinto priest during purification ceremonies; it is made from the sakaki tree and has gohei attached

hatsu-miyamairi: the ceremony of the first visit paid to the local shrine by a newborn baby

hatsu-mōde: the New Year shrine visit

heiden: the shrine building where various religious rites and ceremonies like purification and weddings are performed

himorogi: probably the earliest form of a shrine, consisting of a simple patch of ground marked off by rope and surrounded by evergreen plants and trees

honden: the shrine building containing the symbol of the enshrined kami

ikigami: a "living human kami"; that is, any individual who could be enshrined and worshiped as a kami while still alive

jichinsai: the Shinto groundbreaking ceremony

jingū: a Shinto shrine associated with the imperial family

jinja: the sacred area, usually containing buildings, in which a kami may be worshiped; a general term for a Shinto shrine

kami: a Shinto deity, anything that can inspire in man feelings of awe, reverence, or mystery; not just a divine being but also a tree, a mountain, etc.

kamidana: the "kami" shelf, a miniature Shinto shrine kept for worship inside the home

matsuri: a Shinto festival

-miya: a suffix denoting a Shinto shrine

norito: the liturgical formula spoken at ōbarae and other Shinto purification ceremonies

ōbarae: the ceremony held twice a year at the Meiji Shrine to purify the accumulated transgressions of the nation

oharai: the Shinto purification ceremony

omikoshi: a portable shrine containing the spirit of the local kami; during festivals it is carried through the streets of the town to spread the kami's protection

sakaki: the sacred tree of Shinto, a branch of which is used for the haraigushi

sandō: the main approach road to a shrine

sangaku shinkō: a form of mountain asceticism in which worshipers practice discipline and seek purification in rugged settings

shiki-nen-sengū: the ceremony marking the reconstruction of a shrine and the transference of the kami to the new building

shimenawa: a twisted straw rope hung in front of the home at New Year for good luck and prosperity; also seen at shrines on torii or on buildings

shinshoku: the general term used for a Shinto priest

shintai: the symbol of the enshrined kami; it is kept in the honden

shugendō: general term for the amalgam of Shinto and Buddhism; it was formally abolished in the Meiji period (1868–1912)

temizuya: the stone trough where visitors to a shrine wash their hands and rinse out their mouths before worship

torii: the sacred gateway that stands at the entrance to all shrine precincts

ujiko: all those who are under the patronage of a kami; in effect, the parish community of a shrine

yakubarai: a special Shinto ceremony conducted to calm the spirit of an offended kami

yashiki-gami: a small private shrine kept outside the home

The Tsurugaoka Hachiman Shrine

Japanese Shinto shrines take many different forms. Some take up only as much space as a streetcorner. Others are vast complexes spread out over acres of land, containing several main shrine buildings as well as sub-shrines, worship and entertainment pavilions, and even museums. Tsurugaoka Hachiman Shrine, as an example of the latter, provides a good opportunity to introduce some of the typical features encountered at the more than 100,000 shrines across Japan.

This shrine is of great cultural interest for it is linked with one of the most stirring events in Japanese history—the rise to power of the great warrior Minamoto Yoritomo at the end of the twelfth century. Yoritomo's base of operations was the small seacoast city of Kamakura. There, as undisputed ruler of Japan, he set up his own military government, several hundred miles from the imperial capital of Kyoto. And at the center of his growing city, atop Tsurugaoka Hill, he built a large shrine to honor Hachiman,

Buden. A sacred hall in which ritual dances, music, and ceremonies are performed. This particular *buden* commemorates the dance of Shizuka, the lover of Yoritomo's brother, Yoshitsune. Yoritomo, jealous and suspicious of Yoshitsune, ordered him killed. Shizuka was captured and brought to Kamakura, and upon being ordered to dance did so, but while singing a song in praise of Yoshitsune. As a result, the enraged Yoritomo put her child, a boy, to death.

Gempei Pond. The name of the pond refers to the struggle between Yoritomo's Genji clan and its rival, the Heike. The eastern side contains three islands (the word for "three" in Japanese is *san* and also means "birth"), and the western side contains four islands (*shi* means "four" and "death"). Which side Yoritomo was on should be obvious.

Ginkgo tree. Legend has it that in 1219 the third Kamakura shogun, Sanetomo, was beheaded by his nephew, who had been hiding behind this tree. The tree may not be quite that old, however. But it is a venerable part of the shrine. Old trees at shrines are often festooned with a thick white rope to sanctify the natural spirit within them.

Haiden. One of the main shrine buildings. Ordinary worshipers pay homage here.

Harai-sho. Priests purify themselves here before taking part in ceremonies.

Heiden. One of the main shrine buildings. It is entered only by priests.

Hōmotsuden. The shrine treasure building. Located in the corridor surrounding the main shrine area, it contains possessions of Yoritomo as well as treasures of the Kamakura period (1185–1338).

Honden. Here the *shintai*, or symbol of the enshrined deity, is kept.

Inari Shrine. A sub-shrine that honors the rice deity. It was built several hundred years after the main shrine.

Kokuhōden. Erected by Kamakura City in 1928, the building is modeled on the eighth-century Shōsōin Treasure House in Nara. It contains treasures and important cultural properties of the entire city, both Shinto and Buddhist.

Nōsatsu-sho. This is where pilgrims offer prayers.